I Was Sentenced to Be Shot

Autobiography of a Political Objector

By

MAX SANDIN

Foreword by

RANDY KEHLER

I Was Sentenced to Be Shot

Autobiography of a Political Objector

By

MAX SANDIN

(1889 – 1971)

Original editing by Al Uhrie
1960 – 1963

**Updated and finalized by
Ruth Benn and Ed Hedemann**
2022 – 2024

**Design by
Rick Bickhart**

*We are grateful to Deborah Tenenbaum for permission to publish
her grandfather's story and to Elliot Linzer for indexing this book.*

ISBN 979-8-218-42136-6 (print)
LIBRARY OF CONGRESS CONTROL NUMBER: 2024904313

For Sarah

Contents

continued

Contents

Part Five: War Bound

How a Chance 24-Hour Acquaintance with Max Sandin Changed My Life

By

RANDY KEHLER

I t was a few minutes before midnight on August 27, 1963, a month after my 19th birthday, when I arrived by train from my home in Scarsdale, NY, at the 125th Street train station in New York City and walked half a dozen blocks to the Harlem office of the Congress of Racial Equality, known as "CORE," with a ticket to board a bus bound for Washington, D.C., and the much anticipated and widely publicized March on Washington for Jobs and Freedom.

As I stepped aboard, I could see that the bus was almost totally full, with only one still-empty seat, on the aisle near the front of the bus next to a short, elderly man. When the driver, just before pulling out, briefly switched on all the overhead lights, I could see that this old man and I were the only white persons on the bus.

As soon as I sat down next to him, he turned our overhead light back on and handed me a small, spiral-bound book opened to a page in the middle, saying, "Read this."

Somewhat startled, I immediately started reading it. The little book turned out to be the 1963 desk calendar produced by the War Resisters League, an organization I'd never heard of. The particular page my seatmate had it turned to was entitled, "MAX SANDIN: June 3, 1889–" And underneath that was a four-paragraph "mini-biography" of Max Sandin that read:

In 1910 Max Sandin left his native Russia rather than serve in the Czar's army. In 1918 he was sentenced to be shot for refusing to serve in the American army. His sentence was commuted to 15 years imprisonment and he was eventually released seven months after the War's end, though not until he had been brutally beaten and tortured. During World War II he was one of 16 men over 45 years of age who publicly refused to register under the "older men's draft." Shortly after the first A-bomb was dropped on Hiroshima, he decided to stop paying federal income taxes because most of the revenue is used for military purposes.[1]

The government has harassed Max Sandin intermittently for years by attaching his wages. It has thus succeeded in forcing this peaceful man to "contribute" part of his earnings to the purchase of weapons of annihilation. Sandin, who is partially incapacitated by an accident, retired in 1961 to live out his days on his income from social security — $116 a month, or $3.87 a day. But at this point the government decided to confiscate his pension to satisfy its claims for earlier unpaid taxes. On August 1, 1961, Sandin was notified that his social security check had been turned over to the Internal Revenue Service.

When Sandin went to Washington to protest by sitting down and fasting outside the Secretary of the Treasury's office, he was arrested and confined to a mental ward. He was released after 13 days through the combined efforts of a lawyer, numerous friends, and several pacifists. On arriving home, he was greeted by a notice from the painter's union stating that the government had seized his union pension check.

The People of the United States versus Max Sandin reveals much about a society which demands unquestioning obedience. The action of Max Sandin versus the United States reveals much about the potential of the individual who puts love for his fellow man ahead of money and security.

[1] *Editors' note: Max actually stopped paying taxes in 1943, two years before Hiroshima*

Before we got off the bus in Washington, Max ripped out the page I'd just read and handed it to me. At the top of the page, he wrote: "To Randy Kehler, a Friend of Humanity... Max Sandin." I still have that page and treasure it.

I don't remember what happened next. I'm sure we were both quite tired and probably wanted to get some sleep before our scheduled 8 am arrival in D.C. For my part I was so struck by what I'd read about Max's extraordinary life, that as soon as it began to get light early Wednesday morning and I noticed that Max was awake, I began asking him one question after another about his amazing life and convictions, based on what I'd read.

As I write this now, I can't remember exactly what my questions were, how I worded them, or exactly how he replied. But I do recall that one of the first things I asked him — which, in retrospect, clearly reflected my youth and my unconscious assumption that I myself would someday spend time as a U.S. soldier or sailor — was something like, "Why didn't you want to serve in the Czar's army?" And I remember being deeply moved by his quiet yet immediate, straightforward answer: "Because my mother always taught us that killing was wrong."

I also remember asking him how he managed to get out of Russia and all the way to the U.S. as a very young man from a very poor family. He said something about having made his way out of his native country mostly on foot, hitchhiking rides overland to Germany where he was able to board a cattle boat headed to the United States to stay with a brother in Cleveland.

Though feeling somewhat embarrassed by my ignorance, I also asked him to tell me what he meant by his frequent references to "nonviolence," a term that I didn't think I'd ever heard before — at home, in church, in public school, during my two years at a private high school, nor during my freshman year at Harvard.

I don't remember exactly how Max defined nonviolence, but I'm pretty sure he defined it in very literal terms (at least in the context of human interactions), and very emphatically, as in: *No killing. No intentionally hurting others. No matter what! Period.*

I also asked him, again somewhat embarrassed, what he meant by referring to himself as a "pacifist," a term I'd heard before but only vaguely understood to mean not believing in war. As I recall, Max explained that for him, as for many self-described pacifists, it meant more than not "believing" in war; it also included a hard-and-fast determination never to use guns or other potentially lethal weapons to defend oneself or others, under any circumstances…ever, no matter what.

Then, at the risk of embarrassing myself still further, I asked him what I knew to be the "stock question" often asked of people who claimed to be pacifists (often for the purpose of tripping them up): I said, "So what would you would do if someone was holding a knife to your mother's throat, and you had a gun in your pocket?"

I was sure he'd have an answer, probably confessing that in that kind of situation he'd resort to some kind of non-lethal *physical* violence. But no, without hesitation Max looked at me and quietly answered with words I'll never forget and immediately scribbled down on the calendar page he'd given me: "I can't tell what I *would* do. All I can tell you is what I have done."

His answer to my question stunned me. In the silence that followed that brief exchange I thought, "Wow, if there's anyone whose life experience would allow him or her to say definitively what he or she would probably do, or try to do, in that kind of situation, it would be this quiet old man sitting next to me."

Looking back, I realize that this was, for me, a very early lesson — and a very wise and important one — about the meaning of humility: "Don't be too sure of what you *would* do…until you've *done* it." I've tried to live by that lesson ever since.

There was one other deeply moving thing Max said to me. I don't remember what I must have said that triggered his response, but here's the brief excerpt of our conversation that I scribbled down on the calendar page he'd given to me:

Max: "You have to *fight*…"

Randy: "I *would* fight if I knew what to fight for."

Max: "Just be a human being. That's all."

While I've often wondered what exactly he meant by that, I assume he meant, at the very least: "Human beings don't kill each other."

· · · · ·

I'm pretty sure my further questions and Max's replies ended as soon as we crossed the city limits into Washington. With the sun just beginning to rise over the roofs of block after block of old brick tenement buildings, to my great surprise we could see and hear dark-skinned people leaning out their windows on both sides of the road, exuberantly cheering us on, waving all kinds of sheets, towels, pieces of clothing, etc. To my great surprise — and delight! — people on both sides of the road seemed to be joyously *welcoming* us.

At that point I realized that our bus was part of a whole caravan of buses coming from who-knows-where, some in front of us and many behind us. And it quickly became obvious that all these cheering people knew exactly *why* all of these buses were parading through their neighborhood and that they were *very* glad to see us — almost as though we were an invading army coming to liberate them.

Looking back, now almost 60 years later, I realize that this was one of the most exhilarating moments of my life. And Max seemed really happy, too. It was a moment in time I'll never forget.

· · · · ·

Soon all the buses came to a large parking lot closer to the Capitol and people started getting off. I don't remember whether Max had a walker of some kind or just a cane, but he told me it would take him a few moments to get up and off the bus. Clearly, he had some kind of arthritic type of disability. So, I waited until all the other passengers had disembarked and then took Max's arm to help him get off.

Clearly, he appreciated my assistance and, once on the ground, seemed pleased to continue hanging onto me and having me guide his steps. As we slowly proceeded down a long paved walkway beside the Reflecting Pool toward the Lincoln Memorial, thousands of smiling, cheering, banner-waving black and white marchers were crowded together on both sides of the path, calling out, "Thanks for coming! Freedom Now!" while making sure to leave us space to pass by.

Thanks to their joyful assistance, Max and I were able to make our way up remarkably close to the speakers' platform in front of the Lincoln Memorial, which, by the time we stopped, was just up the steps in front of us, where someone offered a small chair or stool for my elderly partner to sit on.

What an unbelievable thrill this was for me! And, to be sure, for Max, too!

I don't remember too much after that, except that it was a long, hot, but incredibly exhilarating day…and that for hours, which seemed to pass very quickly, we were both riveted on one speaker and entertainer after another, until the final speech by the young Rev. Martin Luther King Jr: his now famous "I Have a Dream" speech, which had the huge crowd cheering non-stop all the way through.

· · · · ·

I would definitely not have predicted at that time, nearly 60 years ago, that I would spend most of the remaining years of my life actively organizing and participating in opposition to U.S. wars and weapons-building, including nuclear weapons. These years included 22-months in prison for noncooperation with the Vietnam draft, 10 weeks imprisonment and the "theft" of my family's home due to my wife's and my refusal to pay federal "war taxes," and shorter incarcerations for trying to shut down our local nuclear power plant.

I can't recall the many instances during this time when I know Max's words and life story came back to me, either initiating or reinforcing my own resolve to take the steps and personal risks necessary in order to resist and noncooperate with U.S. wars and weapons-building.

Yet, as I look back, I know that in a more general sense I often felt, consciously or unconsciously, that I was indeed, in my own way, following in — or at least *trying* to follow in — Max Sandin's big footsteps in opposition to war and killing.

In short, I don't think it would be an exaggeration to say that my 24 hours with Max in August of 1963 have had a profound influence on the rest my life. How could it not?

What a gift his life has been to me…and still is.

Thank you, Max.

Shelburne Falls, Massachusetts
January 2023

For Max Sandin[2]

I cannot cry out for my people
Nor my land, as sang the Psalmist
— I have not people, no land is mine,
And whose God could hear my cries?
What people hear, what God could hear,
Above the roar of machines?
But it will be the cry of all peoples,
Everywhere, together;
And some day they will stop
The machinery, and the people
Will be heard. Those that will hear
Have placed themselves higher than Gods
But because they are not Gods,
They also have fear
And the great cry will shatter at last
The stone that is in their hearts.
And there shall be no nation, no God
Above the people at last,
And the heart of man will be one.

– Jeanne Bagby
a founder in 1961 of Women Strike for Peace

---

[2] *This poem was included in Al Uhrie's edited version of the manuscript.*

INTRODUCTION

"I WAS SENTENCED TO BE SHOT"
                                    BY MAX SANDIN

This is the Story of my life, of my youth
in Russia where I was born, went to Chader, (school)
and later in 1910 Come to the United State Where
I was in 1918 Sentenced to be shot, for refusing
to take a gun, in the First World War.

How I have been tortured, Chained to the
Prison doors for 8 hours a day, Scrubbed with
wire brushes my body. For weeks and months
locked in Solitary confinement. For being a
conscientious Objector against war. But, I hope
that Wars will be abolished from the globe
and this hope, is for me as a torch-bearer
to a world of peace and freedom for all men
humanity.
        I believe, that this story of my life
will be of interest and a great lesson how
we the people of the World can stop War.

Therefore, I wrote this book, I did not
write this book as a Jew or as an American
I write this book only as a human being
for the people all over the world.

Max's original handwritten introduction, 1955.
Courtesy of Western Reserve Historical Society, Cleveland, Ohio.

Part One:
Beginnings

CHAPTER ONE

Under the Czar

I was born June 3, 1889, in Dvinsk (Latvia) Russia. Dvinsk had a population of 60,000, about 75 percent of whom were Jewish. There was a match factory, which employed 1,000 workers, most of them women. There were two tanneries with 1,500 workers, one tile factory employing 600 workers, a railroad engine shop with 3,000 gentile workers, a large knitting industry, and numerous small shops. The revolutionary movement was very strong in the years 1900 to 1910, and it was widely supported by the Jewish workers (the socialist Jewish Labor Bund).[3]

My father was a house painter. He did not work very often because he was nearsighted and could not afford a pair of glasses. At that time, he had to support himself, a wife, and four children. How he did it, I cannot understand. He used to say, "If God gave children, he will take care of them." But he left us to a very stingy caretaker.

[3] *Based on Max's memory; more info on Dvinsk at jewishgen.org/databases/latvia/DvinskFamilies.htm; Max's birth name was probably Mikhail Zarlin but he took the name Max Sandin once in the United States*

Twice a week, my mother used to walk about four miles to the big bazaars, where she would purchase chickens, other fowl, eggs, and pickles, and then she would walk back the four miles to re-sell them to our neighbors for a profit. In this way, she would help my father support the family.

We lived in one room of a six-room house. There were five rooms, each occupied by a different family, and one kitchen shared by all.

The furniture in our room consisted of a couch, a bed, a large cupboard, a table to eat on, four chairs, and two empty beer cartons. At night, we would remove the door to our room and put it down on two chairs, in order to have another place to sleep.

On one side of the kitchen there was a large brick oven, where all the families did their cooking and bread making. Every Friday, my mother and the other women baked *challah* (white bread) for the Sabbath. They used to mark their *challahs* with pieces of eggshell, and the landlady knew each woman's mark.

Under the oven there was a large opening where each family kept a couple of chickens, which supplied them with eggs. On the Day of Atonement, we used these chickens for *kappores* — forgiveness for a year's sins.

During the severe winters, the five or six children in the house stayed in the kitchen all day long and played on top of the huge brick oven. I could not go out because I had no shoes. I remember that we had to clean the chamber pots in the morning while the women cleaned the kitchen. The men of the house would chop wood or transfer it from the shed to the kitchen. Sometimes during the coldest nights, a tenant would bring his horse and cow into the kitchen, where it was warm.

My parents had only one wish in life. My father prayed three times a day that his sons should go to *cheder* to learn Torah, Pentateuch, and to say *Kaddish* at his and our mother's graves for a whole year after they died.

My two brothers did not go to *cheder* because there was no money to pay a teacher. My sister did not go either, not because there was no money to send her (although there wasn't) but because Jewish women were not supposed to go to *cheder* or to attend synagogue. Poor Jews followed this custom very strictly. Of course, rich Jews sent their sons and daughters to *cheder*, schools, and colleges, as they did not care about religion.

About 1895, when I was six years young, my brother Leibe, 14, was working as a painter, and Gabriel, 11, as a shoemaker's apprentice. My sister Sarah, 10, was working too, in a button factory. All in all, the income of the family was a little higher now, so my parents sent me to *cheder*.

I attended *cheder* for nine years. For the first three years I went only in the summer. In the winter, about six months, my father and older brother did not work — so no work, no eat, no shoes, and no *cheder*.

I was a good scholar and willing to learn. My teachers liked me, and they encouraged me. My parents hoped that someday I would become a rabbi, and a big one at that. You could not bargain with them. But at least they were assured of a learned *Kaddish* after they were dead.

One day when I was nine years old, we were reading from the Torah in *cheder* — Samuel I, Chapter 15 — these words of Jehovah: "Now go and smite Amalek, and utterly destroy all that they have, and spare them not; but slay both man and woman, infant and suckling, ox and sheep, camel and ass." I could not understand why Saul was told to destroy infants and sucklings. I knew that grown-ups were killed in wars, but I could not understand why children and young animals had to be killed. I asked my teacher, and his answer was a slap across the face. I lost two teeth, and my mouth was full of blood.

After crying for a few minutes, I asked the Rabbi why he had hit me. He said, "You are not supposed to ask questions on God's words." I think that this incident implanted in me the seeds of conscientious objection to war.

The people of Russia were oppressed, and the Jews were worse off than any other minority. Jews were allowed to live in ten states in Russia, and only within the ghettoes in the cities of those states. Wealthy Jewish merchants could obtain permits to travel and live outside these ghetto states, but they were few in number. Many daughters of rich parents wanted to go to colleges in such cities as Moscow and St. Petersburg. The only way they could was to take out a yellow ticket (passport) — the kinds issued to prostitutes. Prostitutes could move about Russian freely.

The revolutionary movement was very strong among the workers about the turn of the century. When Czar Nicholas II issued a manifesto on October 15, 1905, guaranteeing the people of Russia a liberal constitution which promised inviolability of person, freedom of thought, speech and assembly, the workers and students went out into the streets to demonstrate their happiness. While they were kissing and hugging each other, the Czar's police carefully noted the leaders of the movement. In succeeding weeks, the Cossacks arrested and killed many of the demonstrators.

And if this wasn't enough for the Czar and his Black Hundreds (advisors), the peasants and drifters were told indirectly by the police that they could take from the Jews whatever they wanted, including their lives, without fear of punishment. Many Jews were killed through Russia during this wave of pogroms. In Dvinsk, however, we were lucky. The gentile workers from the tanneries and the railroads distributed a printed leaflet promising that they would protect the Jews from the Black Hundreds. Many of them patrolled the roads leading into the city. The workers knew that the attack on the Jews was an attack on the labor movement as a whole, to divert attention from the revolutionary movement.

Of course, there was friction within Dvinsk between the Jews and the Christians. I remember that several times when my mother was driving geese home the four miles from the bazaar, gentile boys would disperse them with rocks. At times it would take her up to an hour to gather them. Out of spite and with the cruelty of youth, they would yell nasty epithets at my mother, who had only one eye. Sometimes we would wake up in the morning to find a skunk placed in the outhouse.

We Jewish boys would get even, however. We would throw stones at the pigs owned by the gentiles whenever they wandered near us. Sometimes we would go behind the fence and do our natural duty and then take delight in the fact that the pigs, which the Christians were going to eat, would clean it up.

In our ghettoes, very few Jews had occasion to learn to read or write. I was one of the lucky ones who could read books and newspapers which were printed in Jewish without the dots or vowels. As a result, at the age of 14, I became an important spoke in the wheel of the revolution before I knew what I was doing.

On Friday nights, about 10 to 20 young men and women came to my parents' house, and I would read to them socialist pamphlets, brochures, short stories, and books — Marx, Engels, Kropotkin, Bebel, and others. After the reading we would discuss them. The Bund (Jewish socialist movement) leaders considered my readings so valuable that they ordered me not to risk arrest by attending mass meetings or street demonstrations.

One day, when I reached the age of 15, my father called me in and said, "Mikhail, I want to talk to you, man to man. You are a big boy now. Mom and I have done all we can to give you a pious Jewish education, but we cannot do any more. With Leibe in Ekaterinoslav working, and Gabriel in Port Arthur (fighting in the Russo-Japanese War of 1903-04), we can no longer afford to pay for your upkeep. We want you to go to Rabbi Mayer's Yeshiva (Hebrew college), and I will arrange with the head man at the synagogue for you to eat days at strange people's tables. You will be able to come home at night and for the Sabbath."

It was the custom at that time for poor boys who wanted to continue their education to eat "days" — one day a week at a different family's house. Many of these families were also poor with barely enough for themselves. But there was a saying that if you give charity, you will go to heaven. Those families hoped that by helping these boys to study the Talmud and Bible, when they died angel Gabriel would admit them through the gates into heaven. The boys themselves were not always able to find enough families for the number of days in the week. Many of them were from out of town, so they did not eat every day.

I said to my father, "No, I refuse to eat 'days.' I will not take from poor people what they do not have for themselves. I do not want something for nothing."

My father said, with tears in his eyes, "I'm sorry, but you will have to go to Yosel, the shoemaker, as an apprentice for three years. I do not want you to be a painter like I am. Yosel will give you room and board from the first day, and a new pair of high shoes each year."

So, I could not help myself, and a week later I became a shoemaker's apprentice.

Yosel the shoemaker had a wife and six children with another on the way. He had his own house. It was a hole dug in the ground with a roof on it. It had three windows, but the sun's rays never reached them. Inside there were two rooms. One room was the living room, bedroom, and play room — to play in for the little children, and for the grownups to play cards in. There was a bed, two wooden benches, a big wooden table, and eight homemade chairs. On the bed were about ten feather pillows and two bed-sized comforters. It was the custom of Jewish mothers who had girls to accumulate feather pillows as part of their dowry.

At Yosel's house I was more a housekeeper and babysitter than an apprentice. Yosel was very lazy. He played cards and slept in the daytime. He started to work at five in the afternoon and worked till two or three in the morning. I was tired and sleepy, and he beat me more than he fed me. Once he beat me so hard that for three days, I lay on my straw sack (used as a mattress) unable to get up. I could not take it anymore, so I ran away.

My father insisted that I go back to the shoemaker. He was afraid of God, because he had given Yosel his promise that I would stay with him for three years; and a promise by a Jew must be kept, no matter what happens. I went back, but about two months later I got another beating, because he found me reading a book. I was taken to the hospital for a week after this beating. That was the only week in all my years in Russia that I was not hungry and slept in a real bed with white linen.

I did not go back to Yosel, but went to another shoemaker, Reb Simche. He had only two children — a girl and a boy. His wife was a very good woman, and I was treated well. There was only one big room, which served as the living room, bedroom, kitchen, shop, and storage room for wood. The only place for me to sleep was on the flat brick top of the oven. In the summer it wasn't too bad, but in the winter, it was too hot. So, in the winter I slept on the floor with the boy.

I stayed with Reb Simche for two years. I was paid 75 rubles and got my room and board for six days of the week. On Friday nights I went home and stayed over the Sabbath with my parents.

After leaving Reb Simche, I worked in different shops, doing piecework and making about ten rubles a month. I lived with my parents and had my hours to read. I wanted very much to learn how to write Jewish, but I did not have enough money to pay a teacher. Somehow, I managed to study by myself, but I did not make too much progress. Some of my teachers in *cheder* knew how to write Jewish, but they could not afford the time for extra writing lessons.

My parents' hopes and dreams and sacrifices to have a son who would lead them to heaven when they died were not completely lost, at least until my 21st year, when I left home. Never as a boy, nor as a grown-up, did I have a fight. I would not even quarrel with an individual, but only with the capitalistic system.

To please my parents while they were alive, I would wake up every Sabbath at five (after my Bar Mitzvah at 13, when I became a full-fledged Jew) and go to the synagogue with my father and the old Jews. I would teach them from the Holy Scriptures and from the other holy books. That was the dividend that my parents got from their investment in sending me to *cheder*. All the money in the world would not have paid for the joy, pleasure, and happiness that they received from my teaching.

I remember going into the synagogue once on a Monday at the first of the month. The men called me over and asked me what a certain abbreviation on the Calendar of Observances stood for. I told them what it stood for in Hebrew, and then I noticed that my father had started to cry. I asked him why he was crying, and he said that none of the men in the synagogue had known what the initials stood for, and that I, a boy, his son, had known. One of the men had wanted to bet my father five kopecks, which he would not do because he did not believe in betting, but my father would not have exchanged a million dollars for the recognition from his friends that I was a good boy and a good pupil who knew the Bible. He ran home to tell my mother and, from that moment on, I was the talk of the neighborhood.

After I left Russia, however, I never went into a synagogue to pray. I had seen the poverty of my family and our neighbors living four and five families in one house. They had as many children as God wished, and in many homes, God called these children back as soon as they arrived, with others suffering the remainder of their natural, or unnatural lives — many of them with one hand or one leg, mange, leprosy, and many with only one eye. The barbers were also doctors. Very few could afford to call a real doctor in case of illness. The rich people had everything they wished for. They did anything they wanted to do. Many poor servant girls were made pregnant by the sons of the rich and cast into the arms of prostitution. The only consolation the poor had was that their suffering would make them welcome guests in the next world, in heaven, and that the rich would then envy them. This they learned from the rabbis and the rest of the swindlers and religious hypocrites who preached to them.

No, I could not agree with these holy swindlers in the name of a God who did not exist and was only being used as a whip on backward and uneducated people. Synagogues, churches, and temples were places where spiritual poison was being injected into poor human beings (my experience in this country has not changed my opinion).

There is only one belief, and this belief must be practiced in our lives every day, every hour, every minute — love your neighbor as you would yourself, and without exception.

When I was 19, I worked for a shoemaker who had a sister-in-law about 26. She had three assets — a big bosom, a big bank book, and a wish to get married. According to Jewish custom, she was already being called an old maid.

One Saturday night at a party several boys and girls called me over and said, "Mikhail, is it true that you are going to marry Rivka?" I was astonished to hear this and denied it. I went over to Rivka and told her what our friends were saying. Her only comment was, "We'll see tomorrow."

After the party was over, I went back to the shoemaker's place to go to sleep. My bed was my workbench, which was in the living room/kitchen/shop. The shoemaker and his wife slept in the other room, and Rivka in another corner of the room I was in.

In the middle of the night, I felt something pressing against me. I woke up and found another person lying next to me. It was Rivka, naked. She said, "Shhh, Mikhail, keep quiet. I have something to tell you." She kept pressing my head against her bosom. "I have 300 rubles in cash, and I will give you this money. Let's marry tonight, and you will run away to America and then send for me."

I hesitated for a moment at this appealing offer, but I did not know whether I would be any better than some of the other boys who had married, gone to America, and abandoned their wives. I could not do this to Rivka, so I pushed her off the bench. She hurt her knee when she fell and let out a yell. Her brother-in-law and sister woke up and came in with a lamp. Rivka was lying on the floor, naked, with 300 rubles scattered about her. Her brother-in-law and sister didn't say anything, but just looked at her.

I suppose she had told them what she was going to do and that I would be forced to marry her. At this thought, I jumped off the bench, grabbed my clothes and ran away to my parents' house. I never saw Rivka again.

Every boy in Russia had to report to the military for service in the army at twenty-one. If a boy did not report, his parents were fined 300 rubles. If they could not pay, the tax collectors took away everything — clothing, furniture, bedding, and even the candlestick, a most precious possession of Jews, which was lit Friday nights in honor of the Sabbath.

Many boys cut off fingers or went to the dentist to have some of their teeth extracted, in order not to serve in the army. Some Jewish boys did this because they felt it was against their religion, and they knew that in the totalitarian army of the Czar they would have to violate countless Jewish customs and laws, such as eating food that wasn't kosher.

My parents were upset, not merely for religious reasons, but because my brother Gabriel had been reported missing in the Russo-Japanese War. I did not want to perpetuate the Czar's cruel and unjust reign.

We talked about my going to America. The only way I could do this without having my parents' meagre possessions taken from them would be to register for the army, take the loyalty oath, and then run away after having spent 24 hours in the army. My brother Leibe had done this, and when he offered to finance my trip to America where he was, I decided upon this course of action.

CHAPTER TWO

America

Max Sandin circa 1910s. Photo courtesy of Deborah Tenenbaum.

About October 10, 1910, a few days after I was officially inducted into the czarist army, I ran away from Dvinsk. For two days, I was one of nine men and three women in the hands of an agent who led us across Russia to the German border. We slept during the day and walked or sometimes crawled on all fours during the night until we arrived at the city of Grajewo, where we crossed the German border at 2 o'clock in the morning.

For three days we were confined to a two-story building under quarantine. Then one morning we were told to board the steamship *Brandenburg* at Bremen. We were on the ocean 14 days. Many of us were homesick, and the rest were seasick. It was a cattle boat, and I am sure that the cattle had a more enjoyable voyage than the passengers. We arrived in Philadelphia on November 12th, and the next day I traveled across Pennsylvania and Ohio to Cleveland.

My older brother Leibe Zelig [aka Louis Sandin] lived at 3131 Scovill Avenue in a four-room suite. There was a living room, two bedrooms, a large kitchen, gas, and electricity — all this for one family! He had a wallpaper and paint store in the front. I was made welcome by my brother, sister-in-law, and two beautiful nieces.

I had brought a pair of silver candlesticks, as a present from my mother to her daughter-in-law, to be used on Friday nights when the candles were lighted for the Sabbath. In my travel box, I had a phylactery to pray with — a gift from my pious father — but I never used it.

A few days after my welcome as a guest, my brother asked me what I was going to do. I said that I would like to work at the painting trade temporarily and go to night school to take up a profession. My brother and sister-in-law did not approve of this. They advised me not to become a painter, but a peddler instead. I told them that I did not like the idea of buying and selling. I wanted to be a worker, not a businessman.

Against my better judgment, I yielded to my brother who took me to a 5- and 10-cent store and bought me a suitcase for 65 cents and filled it with gas mantles, shoelaces, soap, washcloths, needles, and other household items.

The next day I was told to board a Scovill Avenue streetcar and ride to a Polish and Russian neighborhood at the end of the line.

I worked until four p.m., and for six hours of work I made a profit of $1.65.

In the first day as a peddler, I made more than an experienced painter (the union wage of a painter was $2.00 a day or 25 cents an hour), but I did not like it.

The following day, I went out at nine in the morning and came back at four. I had sold all my wares and had made a profit of $2.25. I said, "No more," and threw away my suitcase. That was my second and last day as a businessman.

A week after I became an apprentice painter and paperhanger for my brother. I was accepted as a member of the Painters' Union, Jewish Local 123, District Council 6. (In February, 1913, the Jewish Local 123 was dissolved because the business agent, Brother Miller, had made a settlement with the contractors for an increase of two-and-a-half-cents an hour, as had Locals 128 and 129, so the leadership of the union, in Lafayette, took away our charter for protesting and transferred the members to other locals. I was transferred to Local 128.)

About two weeks after I started at the painting trade and the important question of how to make a living was settled, I went to night school. Most of the students were beginners — young boys and girls, immigrants from Russia, Poland, Latvia, Lithuania, and a few from Palestine. About 85 percent of them were Jewish.

I liked to study and, as in *cheder*, I was one of the best in spelling, reading, and grammar. My hopes were very high. They reached to an office in the highest building as a big lawyer, or at least in a smaller office as a good dentist. But I sidetracked both offices and remained a house painter and paperhanger — loyal to my class as a worker.

I finished elementary school and later went to Central High School. For two semesters, I attended a technical high school for architecture. At the same time, I attended Hebrew school for two winters.

After I was in this country three months, I got my first citizenship papers. I became a member of the Socialist Party on May Day 1911. (In April 1916, I got my second papers.)

In the spring of 1913, when the painting season started, I asked my brother for a raise of $3 a week. He paid me $12 a week for 6 days work. He said I wasn't worth any more, and if I don't like it, I could look for another job with more money.

I saw an ad in the *Cleveland Press* for a paperhanger for Mr. Westropp on West 25th Street. I took the job. At that time all the paperhangers were working piecework at 25 cents a double roll. I started Thursday from noon until 4:30, then worked Friday and Saturday 8 hours a day. At 4:30 on Saturday I put in my slip to get paid $13.25 for hanging 106 rolls of paper. I was paid in full without a word said. I worked in this shop for seven months until November.

In April 1914 I partnered with Max Mironoff, a painter, good mechanic, and an honest man. We got a contract from a builder to paint and paperhang three houses for $900. My partner did the inside painting and I did the paperhanging and helped him with the outside painting. We made $28 a week. The official union wages were $20 a week, so we made good.

We also had a few alteration jobs where we made a few extra dollars above the union wages. I was very satisfied to go on like this. But one day my partner said to me, "Max, I would suggest that we shall go out and look for more work, hire painters who will help us, and we will pay them union wages." "No!" I said, "I do not want to make any profit from any man. I am a socialist. I try to do the best and all I can to abolish the present capitalist system. I do not want to be a big contractor."

In 1914 I also went to work for Moses Halper, a builder of many houses all over town, but only as a paperhanger. Because of my Painters' Union activities, I was blackballed by all the Jewish contractors and could not get a job. So, I worked for him about four years until I was drafted to go to ... prison. One day, Mr. Halper said, "Max, we opened a new subdivision on Kinsman Road about three miles from Woodland Avenue in the Jewish neighborhood. I wish that you should become a real estate salesman and sell my lots in the new Mount Pleasant subdivision. And to start, I will give you a $200-lot for $100." I replied, "Thank you but I don't want to be a salesman. I want to work for my money." He replied, "Max, you are an honest fool, will you take the lot for $100?" I agreed. This way I became a property owner and a small part of the capitalist system.

One of my friends, Sam Goldstein, bought a lot next to mine for $200. In 1916 Goldstein and I became partners in real estate. We sold one lot and on the other we built a two-story, two-family house with five rooms each .... Building the house cost us $5,200 and my investment was in the painting of it.

Many social clubs were organized without any real purpose, just for good times. I got together with a few boys and girls, members of the Socialist Party, and we organized an August Bebel (German socialist writer) Club, the aim of which was to prepare members for the Socialist Party. Our slogan was "Dancing, Lectures, and Ice Cream." We were very successful, and in a short time we absorbed two other clubs. In 24 months, we had 65 members. On May Day 1912, four members of the August Bebel Club made out applications to join the Socialist Party.

> *I got together with a few boys and girls and organized an August Bebel Club to prepare members for the Socialist Party. Our slogan was "Dancing, Lectures, and Ice Cream."*

About 1913,[4] the Young People's Socialist League (YPSL) was organized in New York City. Two months later the August Bebel Club became a branch of YPSL, with a membership of 100. I was elected organizer.

The Jewish Branch of the Socialist Party opened a library on East 39th Street and Woodland Avenue. We had about 800 books. YPSL was in charge of the rooms, books, key, dust, and dirt. The library was open on Friday night, and all day Saturday and Sunday. During the week, the library was closed because everybody was working (or supposed to be working). And weeknights we went to night school. The married men were busy with their wives, or the other way around.

As the library rooms were empty most of the time, the dirt and dust accumulated. Dora Sacheroff and I had the honor of being a committee to come Friday evening and clean up and dust. We did our dirty duty cheerfully.

The Young Peoples was a very active group. We often arranged lectures with Max Hayes, editor of the *Cleveland Citizen*, which was the official paper of the Cleveland Federation of Labor. We also had as our lecturers Professor Douglas, Victor Berger, Meyer London, Mayor Hohn, Charles Ruthenberg, Eugene Debs, Peter Witt, and a great number of Jewish lecturers and writers.

We also had good times arranging parties, banquets, dances, and picnics. At that time not many had cars, so we ordered special street cars, stopping at East 55th and Scovill Avenue. (Our library had moved to 5610 Scovill Avenue, where the Socialist Party had bought a house for a Labor Lyceum.) For about three years we had had our yearly picnic at Bedford Glens. Once the members wanted to go

---

[4] *Founded in Chicago in 1907, then in New York City under a slightly different name, and they eventually united.*

to a new picnic place, so they elected Comrade Herzog and myself to find a new place. We went to the streetcar company to inquire about a new place, but there was none. So, I ordered a special car for Bedford Glen again but reported to the members that "This year we are going to Cheerful Lake."

The members wanted to know where Cheerful Lake was, but we told them it would be a surprise. On the day of the picnic many members arrived too late to take the special car, so they went downtown to inquire how to get to Cheerful Lake. They were told that there was no such amusement place in or around Cleveland but that a social car had left for Bedford Glens. When we and they arrived at Bedford Glens, they wanted to throw me into the lake, but I was pardoned for being such a kissable organizer.

In 1916, when President Wilson proclaimed a Jewish Relief Day for the war sufferers in Europe, the Peoples Relief Committee organized a big bazaar. YPSL, with its 200 members, supported this action on all fronts. We collected clothes, shoes, furniture, toys, stoves, and many more articles. We helped sell them, we served as waiters, did K.P. — there were no jobs too big for us to do. We sent out 100 couples on Relief Tag Day to collect money in the streets. We volunteered as collectors to pick up the weekly pledges. On Sunday mornings, when I went to collect in my district, the kids used to shout, "Mom, the war man is coming."

In 1917, because I was working at jobs all over town, I was persuaded to buy a car, a Ford Model T but without a starter and without demountable rims. It cost me $360. I had $160 and got a $200 loan from Morris Plan Bank for the rest. So now I became a full-fledged capitalist. But for all my possessions, I worked for them without exploiting another human being.

After I bought the car, I announced to YPSL members, "Any member for the past three years who pays up their dues will get a ride in my new car." Within the two months we collected $89 in dues from 123 members. However, some of the members got cold feet and were afraid to take a chance to go with me in the new car, especially with the *new* driver. They were not fools.

On East 46 Street and Woodland Ave., in the heart of the Jewish neighborhood, there was an old stone church with six long steps to walk up. In the night, the church was dark but by 9:30 pm when all the night school students came out, the church steps were busy as Wall Street in New York; you could not get a seat;

it was like an Arabian bazaar. There were dates, appointments, spelling lessons, love lessons, too.

Across the street from the church was an old brick building that had a wine bar in the basement with a couple dirty tables and benches. One Saturday evening, six boys invited me to go with them for a glass of wine. I never smoked or drank but this time it would not look good if I were to refuse. They ordered two quarts of wine. I had one glass but couldn't drink any more. They laughed and joked about me for not drinking more.

Then I heard voices of two young women with their husbands coming down the stairs out of curiosity. I was ashamed to meet them in such a filthy place, so Hertzog and I ran to the lavatory and bolted the door. I sent out a note telling them, "It is a shame for young ladies to come to a place like this," but I didn't sign my name. They recognized my handwriting and called "Sandin and Hertzog, come out from the stinky room." Herzog left but I remained for two hours until the young couples left. Until today — now 40 years later — they are not sure that Max Sandin, organizer of YPSL, was in that stinky room. If they ever read this, they will know it was I, and that I acted properly.

In the course of time, we did our duty to the community to enlarge the population of our city and country. About 40 marriages were the outcome of the political, economic, and social relations of the youth of the YPSL, and I had the best luck of all. I picked the most intelligent and good looking, and the one who spoke the most languages, Jewish, Polish, Russian, and English. She didn't say "No" in any of them. Sarah Madow and I were married on August 28, 1920.

Part Two:
The
"Great" War

CHAPTER THREE

I Will Not Take a Gun

I n 1910, I had left Russia, my home, my beloved parents, and friends, because I did not want to spend many years of my life in the army of the Czar. My brother had been killed in the Russo-Japanese War of 1903-04 and I was well acquainted with the ways of the army because, in my city of Dvinsk, there had been a standing army of several thousand men, many of them quartered in private homes.

These were among the reasons why I was glad and proud to become a citizen of the United States in 1916. I promised to protect the Constitution, including the liberties guaranteed by the Bill of Rights. Here, at last, I felt I was in a country where the dictates of one's conscience would be honored, and where one would not be dragged off to the army to kill.

When the United States declared war against Germany in 1917, and a compulsory draft law was enacted which subjected all young men to service in the army, I felt as if I were back again in Czarist Russia.

I, as a human being, was against killing my fellow men and, as a class-conscious worker, was against war because I believed it was the product of the profit system, arranged by governments for the benefit of unscrupulous capitalists. I knew that the people of the world did not want and have never wanted war.

On April 7, 1917, the day after war was declared, the executive committee of the Socialist Party met in emergency session in St. Louis. The Party went on record against the war and issued the following statement:

> The Socialist Party of the United States in the present grave crisis reaffirms its allegiance to the principle of internationalism and working-class solidarity the world over, and proclaims its unalterable opposition to the war just declared by the government of the United States....
>
> The mad orgy of death and destruction which is now convulsing unfortunate Europe was caused by the conflict of capitalist interest in the European countries.
>
> In each of these countries the workers were oppressed and exploited. They produced enormous wealth but the bulk of it was withheld from them by the owners of the industries....
>
> The capitalist class of each country was forced to look for foreign markets to dispose of the accumulated "surplus" wealth....
>
> The efforts of the capitalists of all leading nations were, therefore, centered upon the domination of the world markets....
>
> This led to the mad rivalry of armament.... The ghastly war in Europe was not caused by an accidental event, nor by the policy or institutions of any single nation. It was the logical outcome of the competitive capitalist system....
>
> Our entrance into the European War was instigated by the predatory capitalists of the United States who boast of the enormous profit of $7 billion from the manufacture and sale of munitions and war supplies and from the exportation of American foodstuffs and other necessaries....
>
> We brand the declaration of war by our government as a crime against the people of the United States and against the nations of the world....[5]

We had endless discussions in the Young Peoples Socialist League as to the best approach to the draft. Some of us agreed with Eugene Debs that one should not

---

[5] *Full text – https://www.marxists.org/history/usa/parties/spusa/1917/04-war-proclamation.htm*

register but should go to jail. I was in a group that believed that as citizens we should obey all civilian laws, including registration, but when we received our first military command, we should refuse to carry it out.

Late in 1917, I received a notice to report for registration. At the draft board I told the clerk that I was an objector to war on political grounds (at that time I was not a pacifist and knew little about pacifism). He asked me if I had ever peeled potatoes. I said no. "Well, you will peel them in the army," he replied.

On May 29, 1918, at 11 pm, we, a group of eight boys — members of YPSL — with about 30 friends, went to the old Union Station. We, the guiltless, harmless, frightful young men, were piled into eight box cars – 40 men in each — on a cattle train. Our friends were left behind with tears in their eyes. I took no baggage, because I did not expect to stay long.

We traveled on the box train for 48 hours until we arrived at Camp Gordon, Georgia. The food on the train consisted of meatless bread sandwiches with cream-less cold coffee. We had no sleep for two nights. The corporal in charge, who wore a civilian suit, was one of the drafted men but the language — I never heard so many foul adjectives! I suppose he was born and raised in the United States Army.

We did nothing the first day except talk among ourselves. On the next day (June 2), many were so tired that they couldn't get up. A uniformed sergeant came in and ordered, "Everybody, go outside now!" I was thinking shall I start or wait, but the sergeant didn't wait. He grabbed me by my arm and pushed me out. We were now in a large open field and, as a corporal yelled "Attention!" the captain came over, pointing to some tents across the way. "Over there is a group of soldiers who are the best and bravest in the United States Army. But I am warning you not to have any contact with them, they are a herd of S.O.B.s. I will court-martial anyone caught talking or dealing with the black bastards. Remember that."

Now, I made up my mind, I am not going to be a soldier.

"I hope there are no conscientious objectors in my company," the captain announced the next evening at retreat. "But if there are, raise your goddamn hands."

I started to shiver. Several of my friends from Cleveland who had reported to the Camp with me asked me if I was sick. I could not answer them. I knew what I had to do. Finally, I managed to raise my hand.

The captain informed me (I felt as if I were the only one who had raised his hand) that I was to report to his office after supper.

When I returned to the barrack several of the draftees who had seen me raise my hand gathered around my cot. One of them struck me on the head. Then they all joined in a rain of fists. I heard someone yell, "Kill that goddamn Jew-objector," "Let's string him up," and "Where's the rope?"

Just as I thought the end was approaching, the draftees snapped to attention. An officer had entered the barrack. He looked at me. My clothes were torn; I was bloody. He turned to the draftees and then apologized. But not to me. "Boys," he said, "I am sorry. I'm afraid I came in too early."

I decided to be a free man and not to be a slave or a brave soldier in an unknown grave.

After dinner I went to the captain's office and was happy to see what seemed like several hundred conscientious objectors waiting to be interviewed. That night I heard about 200 men had raised hands, but most were religious objectors while I am a political objector.

When my turn came, the captain questioned me about my beliefs. One of the questions, which turned out to be quite popular in succeeding months, was: "What would you do if the Germans came over here and raped your sister or mother?"

The following morning, we were supposed to pick up uniforms and guns. I knew that the moment was rapidly approaching when I would be directly confronted with a military command. Instead of going to the quartermaster, I ran over to the captain's office. My hair was all messed up, and I must have looked like a crazy man.

"Where is the captain?" I yelled. "I want to see the captain."

A lieutenant commanded me to come to attention, but I paid him no heed.

"I want to see the captain."

Finally, someone said, "I am the captain."

I sat in a chair, but the lieutenant ordered me to stand up. I could not. I told the captain that I did not want a uniform, and I would not take a gun. The captain told me to be calm, I told him again that I did not want a uniform or a gun.

"I order you to," he said.

"No, I will not."

At this point the captain commanded the lieutenant to take me to the wardroom to get me a uniform and a gun.

There the clerk made a bundle and presented it to me with a gun.

"I will not take them," I said.

"I order you to take them," the lieutenant insisted.

I stood mute and motionless.

"You refuse to obey my order," he queried threateningly. "Do you know what will happen to you if you do not obey my order?"

"I don't care."

The lieutenant summoned two guards and had me taken to the guardhouse.

It was about noon when I was placed in a big empty barrack. A little later the guards brought in a bundle containing a uniform; they forcibly stripped me. Outside of the barracks were puddles of water from a recent rain. I threw the bundle into a puddle.

The room contained only an iron bed with an iron spring. There was no mattress, no toilet, water, or lights. I remained there, alone, a prisoner, for the rest of the day and night.

A lieutenant came into the room the next morning with a gun, some rags, and a bottle of polish. "Here's your gun," he said. "I want you to clean it, and I want you to do a perfect job of it."

I would not take the gun.

"I am not giving you the gun for keeps," he said, trying to reason with me. I just want you to clean it."

"I will not take a gun."

"Do you refuse to take it?"

"I refuse."

At this point he gave me a copy of the Army's rules and regulations and told me to read it, especially Article 64, because I would need it. He left with the gun.

Article 64 said that anyone who willfully disobeys a lawful command of his superior shall suffer death or such other punishment as a court-martial may direct.

For two days and nights, I received no food or water. On the third day of my imprisonment, a lieutenant came in with two guards. He gave me a bundle containing a pair of ordinary pants and an old shirt. I put them on. They took me to the mess hall for breakfast, but I told them that I would not eat until I washed myself. There had been no water or toilet facilities in the barracks. The guards took me to the shower.

Some of my YPSL friends had seen me in the mess hall, so they came down to the shower with a razor for me. They wanted to know all that had happened. Some of them agreed that I had done the right thing. Others warned me to take back my statement. They said they saw a clipping in the mess hall that told of two conscientious objectors who had each received sentences of 45 years.

"See what will happen to you," one of my friends said. "Say you made a mistake, Max, before it's too late." But I couldn't.

On the table back in the mess hall, I found a full plate of pancakes, syrup, and a big pot of coffee — my first meal in two days. The mess hall sergeant teases, "If you had some brains, you'd be on shooting range where the men are practicing with their guns. Within 10 days they leave for Europe to kill Germans. And you will rot in prison while they are having a good time with German Frauleins."

One Sunday, while eating breakfast, the army chaplain gave us a speech saying we are in war and we should not waste any food; whatever is left from breakfast you will have at dinner. "You men shall remember and obey this order." Two days later while on K.P. duty in the officers' dining hall, there were dozens of empty whiskey, beer, and champagne bottles, as well as 10-pound chunks of beef, dozens of barely touched pies, many pounds of vegetables that were wasted under the tables. Women of the soldiers who lived in the camps used to come with their small children to pick through the garbage cans for food.

On June 9, 1918, I was called into the main office and a man gave me his card, saying, "My name is Klein. I am a lawyer. Your brother sent me here to investigate the case and to defend you." I thanked him, telling him that I did not commit any crime and do not need a defender. "I am old and big enough to take care of myself." The lawyer did not like it but he went back to Cleveland anyway.

Back in the guardhouse I found that I had been joined by two

more prisoners. The sergeant told us to get some tools and go into the street to shovel horse shit. I was not sure whether to work or not, but I decided to work, reasoning that I would be able to see my friends and find out what was going on in the camp.

While we were working in the street, I heard a voice saying, "Look, there's Max Sandin, the organizer of the Young Peoples' Socialist League from Cleveland." I looked up and saw the two Gibbs brothers from Cleveland. The other brother responded, "We came with him on the same train only four days ago and he's in prison already? No wonder. He is the organizer of YPSL, what did you expect from him? He did his duty." That was the best compliment I ever heard about myself. I felt very much satisfied at that moment.

For two days I shoveled manure. On the third day two guards took me to chop wood. On the way out to the woodpile one of the guards said to me "You see, nobody is in the camp now. If you were a good boy, you would be out there on the rifle range with the others learning how to shoot."

When we arrived at the woodpile one of the guards left and the other one started to talk with me, even though this was forbidden. He said that I didn't have to work. All I had to do was stay there. He told me that he was a draftee with a wife and child. He would like to be doing the same thing that I was doing, but he said he did not have the courage. After a half hour the other guard came back as a replacement. In private, he told me about the same thing the other soldier had. I worked on the woodpile for four days, and I did as much work as the guards.

About the fifteenth of June, while I was cleaning the streets, one of the new guards said, "Pick up all your belongings. We have a long way to go." I said that I have nothing to take. Another guard handcuffed my wrists to make sure I would not attack them. I walked with a guard on either side of me for about an hour, then they stopped to tie me to a tree with a rope, saying, "Wait here and don't run away."

After an hour, the guards came back with another prisoner, who they handcuffed to me and we started walking again, but stopped again after 45 minutes. As there were no trees, they handcuffed our feet together, telling us to stay there and wait for their return.

About 8 pm, the guards returned with two new men. By 9:30 it was dark when we reached a small town where the guards took us to a restaurant for supper. Afterwards, we walked again, eventually arriving in Atlanta where we were taken to the city jail and locked up for the night while the guards went to a hotel.

Here in our new overnight "motel," we were surrounded by stone walls, iron bars, and beastly guards, handcuffed hands and feet. We could not sleep, so each of us told his story. One worked as a salesman in a New York fish store, was a U.S. citizen and had no schooling. He raised his hand as a conscientious objector because he saw that other men had raised their hands. Seven weeks later he was sent home as mentally deficient. Another was a very smart man, on the executive committee of the Socialist Party. Later he accepted noncombatant service and got an easy job.

At 8 am, the guards returned and marched us to a restaurant for breakfast. At 9 am we boarded a train again, destination unknown. About 3 pm we stopped at Kansas City, Kansas, and went to a restaurant for lunch. I ordered a steak, which was the only decent dinner I had in the last three weeks. At 4 pm we were on the train again and one of the guards remarked, "It won't take long now."

CHAPTER FOUR

Fort Leavenworth

Leavenworth U.S.D.B. building circa 1918. Photo courtesy of Swarthmore College Peace Collection.

About two hours and 40 miles further, we found our-selves in Fort Leavenworth, Kansas. Here we were in front of the big, dreadful, horrible prison known as the United States Disciplinary Barracks (U.S.D.B.), a 10-story building plus basement and a sub-basement with armed guards patrolling day and night. It was surrounded by a cement fence two feet thick and 20 feet high with a large iron gate and heavy doors that make you shiver. My heart started to pound like the wheels of the train that brought us here. My knees were trembling and I could not walk but I dragged them. I was thinking to myself, "Goodbye free world, goodbye to all my friends, I may not see you anymore." But I was really glad that I was not on the battlefield with a gun on my shoulder.

> *The large iron gate with heavy doors makes you shiver. My heart started to pound like the wheels of the train that brought us here. My knees were trembling. I was thinking to myself, goodbye free world.*

We were escorted to the executive offices, where our papers were given to a Colonel Rice. "Get out of here you sons of bitches," the colonel shouted. The guards were confused and scared but ventured to explain that the papers said to deliver us to Fort Leavenworth.

"They don't belong here," the colonel said, "Take them down to the fort headquarters."

When I heard those sweet words, "They don't belong here," I felt as if I had a new lease on life.

(Fort Leavenworth was a regular army base while the U.S.D.B. at Fort Leavenworth was a military prison. Neither of these should be confused with the civilian federal prison which is also located in Leavenworth, Kansas.)

By the time we arrived at the fort headquarters, I had developed cramps from my steak dinner. I asked an orderly for something for my stomach. The orderly told an officer, who told him to take me to the hospital.

I was left waiting on a bench in the hospital. Finally, I walked over to the desk and asked if there was anything wrong. "I have been waiting here for two hours," I said, "and nobody is paying any attention to me." The clerk said he had orders to keep me there.

After what seemed an eternity, I was taken down to a ward, where I received a pair of pajamas, a bathrobe, and slippers.

The next day I did nothing. The patients would not talk to me but only gave me dirty looks. On the third day of my stay in the hospital, several doctors came in and one of them said: "Private Sandin, we would like to examine you. Do you have any objections?"

"Do what you please," I answered. "But, please, I am not a private. I am not in the army." They examined me from top to bottom, and then disappeared. I did not see them again until two days later, when they came back and questioned me about my life, my sisters, my brothers, my parents, my grandparents, aunts, uncles, etc. One doctor asked me how I was with women. I told him that I had never had intercourse with a woman.

"Why? You are a strong, healthy man!"

I told him that I was a socialist, and we were trying to make this a better world. Prostitution was a product of the present system. If I did not want my sister or my sweetheart or my mother to be a prostitute, how could I be consistent if I took advantage of other women?

One of the doctors said to the others that he had found nothing wrong with me. Another commented that I had a strong character.

The next day one of the doctors stopped by my bed and said to me in Yiddish: "Mr. Sandin, I suppose you want to go home."

"Positively."

"Then I advise you to make a statement that someone in your family had been in an insane asylum."

I said, "Thank you, but I want to go home as an honest man."

That was the end of my visits with the doctors.

The patients remained unfriendly toward me. Once when I was sitting on the steps, someone dumped a bucket of garbage over me from the window above.

An orderly asked me if I would sweep out the rooms. I did so, to relieve the boredom, but after a few days I told him I did not like the job. He said that if I did not like it, they had another job for me. I was sent to the venereal-disease ward, where my duty was to see that the patients took their treatments. There I found soldiers who had contracted venereal disease in beds surrounded by wire cages, so they would have no contact with one another. They ate from paper plates. Each patient had a little burner, over which he was to heat a wire. When the wire was red hot, he was to dip it into a bottle of medicine and push it into his penis. When I saw this, I ran away and did not come back to work.

I remained in the hospital for several weeks, doing nothing. Meanwhile, I learned from other C.O.s who had come to the hospital that quite a few C.O.s had arrived at the fort and were quartered together. I decided that I wanted to be with them.

Because they had taken my clothes away from me when I entered the hospital, I went to the post headquarters in my pajamas. A startled captain asked what I was doing there and where my clothes were. Finally, he called out to the C.O.s, "Does anybody have a pair of pants for Max?" Somebody gave me a pair — size 42 (my size was 36) — an old shirt, and a pair of shoes.

CHAPTER FIVE

A Significant Pile of Rubbish

Max Sandin at Fort Riley September 17, 1918. Photo courtesy of Deborah Tenenbaum.

Shortly thereafter, I was taken to Fort Riley, which was about a hundred miles west in the heart of Kansas. I found that over a hundred C.O.s had been transferred there from Fort Leavenworth. They were all types — from primitive religious sectarians to atheists and socialists.

Before I arrived, these men had been asked to build a cantonment for themselves, to clear a field, dismantle, move and re-erect two barracks, construct a latrine, and install a plumbing and drainage system. Most of the men had refused to do this work. They reasoned that the government was holding them against their will and that they should either be freed, imprisoned, or cared for while they were being detained. Also, they knew that the cantonment would probably be used for military purposes after they left.

One of the sore spots had been the fact that the men had to do K.P., not only for themselves, but for noncommissioned officers and noncombatant C.O.s. When about half of the group refused one evening, they were marched out to a lot which contained a single pump for water, and nothing else. They were given tents to erect and were told that if they wanted to eat, they would have to walk a half mile each mealtime to pick up raw rations, walk back the half mile to the pump for water and wood, and then walk a little farther to a spot where they could build a fire to prepare their food individually.

Evan Thomas, Howard Moore, and Harold Studley Gray went on a hunger strike to protest these orders. After three days, the officers gave in and provided the C.O.s with a field kitchen and raw rations. Many of the men did not want to prepare their own food, believing that the government should provide them with cooked rations while they were being detained. Other C.O.s, however, decided to prepare food both for themselves and for the absolutists.

When I arrived at Fort Riley, I did K.P. for a few meals. I saw the vast difference in the rations provided the enlisted men and C.O.s on the one hand and the officers on the other. The former received unappetizing staples and watery coffee while the officers had choice cuts of meat, cognac, wines, and other drinks. I stopped doing K.P. and was transferred to the tent colony (as the lot was called).

A colonel from Washington came to investigate conditions at the camp, apparently because of a telegram sent by several of the socialists. Our food had to be prepared under the hot sun and was constantly besieged by swarms of flies, which alternated between our food and the raw sewage. Sanitary conditions did not exist. He assured us that the situation was only a temporary one and that although we were under guard and unable to leave the lot, we were not prisoners. This restriction was rescinded after the colonel left.

Despite not having seen women for 6 to 8 months, one day (during the fifth day of a hunger strike) a doctor with four soldiers came to our tent. A soldier shouted, "Attention!" but no one stood up. The doctor said, "We are here for a 'short-arm inspection.' Do you have anything against it?" One of the men said, "Go ahead and do it but we will not cooperate." The doctor started to unbutton the pants of the first man, who was in the bed nearest the door, and examined his penis. He spent about an hour examining, talking, brooding, and swearing but none of the eight of us said a word. As he was leaving, the doctor remarked, "You goddamn mute animals are too smart to be soldiers. You should all be shot."

> *"You goddamn mute animals are too smart to be soldiers. You should all be shot."*

One night a big storm broke out and tore away all the tents, followed by a torrential rain. When our tent was blown down, the center pole fell and hit me on the upper lip. I needed to see a doctor but the rain was too strong. All night we suffered with no help until morning. When I went to the hospital, the doctor put seven stitches on my upper lip creating a scar that I still have.

Friction developed between those of us who would not prepare our own food and those C.O.s who prepared it for us. Eventually, some of the men went out on a hunger strike until the government would prepare the food for them. The C.O. cooks became so upset that we wouldn't do noncombatant service to the extent of preparing our own food that they went out on strike.

Evan Thomas, Howard Moore, Harold Gray, and Erling Lunde decided to go on a fast for liberty. In their letter to Secretary of War Newton D. Baker they said: "We understand that the government is not prepared to exempt conscientious objectors from compulsory service. We have therefore determined to refuse to eat as long as we are kept from following the pursuits we feel called upon to follow in life. We fully realize the gravity of this stand, but we are determined to starve rather than passively submit to an act which we believe to be opposed to the principles which we hold dearest in life."

These men decided to abandon their fast on the thirteenth day, after War Department representatives, who had been applying pressure on them, assured them that matters would be brought to a head, that conditions in the tent colony would improve, that their segregation would be ended, and that absolutists would be court-martialed.

While we were having our troubles in the tent colony, I learned that seven men, whom I got to know quite well later at Camp Funston, were being tortured inside of the Fort Riley Guardhouse. Here is an excerpt from the diary of Charles Larsen, one of the seven (the others were Mayer Bernstein, Benjamin Breger, Julius R. Greenberg, Herman Kaplan, Francis X. Hennessey, and Rexford Powell):

> On Sunday morning, August 25, 1918, about nine o'clock the prison sergeant and a lieutenant, the "officer of the day," came to the solitaries and took three of our seven men (namely, Herman Kaplan, Benjamin Breger and Francis Hennessey), one at a time, into the corridor; a hemp rope slung over the railing of the upper tier was put about their necks, hoisting them off their feet until they were at the point of collapse. Meanwhile the officers punched them on their ankles and shins. They were then lowered and the rope was tied to their arms, and again they were hoisted off their feet. This time a garden hose was played on their faces with the nozzle about six inches from them, until they collapsed completely, when they were carried and dumped screaming and moaning into the cage and dumped into bed. The next day the officers were transferred with their company to another post.

These men had been classified by the Board of Inquiry as either "sincere," and therefore eligible for noncombatant service, or "insincere," and required to do combatant service. I think they proved their mettle and sincerity, however, in refusing to undertake either combatant or noncombatant service and by the tortures they underwent here and later in Camp Funston.

I later learned that Evan Thomas (brother of Norman Thomas) had been court-martialed on September 17th for refusing to eat when ordered to do so on his hunger strike. He received a life sentence (the prosecutor had asked for death), which was commuted through "clemency" of the court martial to twenty-five years.

One afternoon, the new post commander, Colonel Waterman, came to speak to us. We were ordered to stand in formation, which we refused to do. He told us that we had to accept noncombatant service, and he read a communique from President Wilson detailing the various kinds of noncombatant service.

One of the C.O.s asked the colonel a question, but the colonel snapped back that President Wilson was the only man doing any thinking these days and that he was thinking for all of us.

Colonel Waterman told us that he would give us until the next day to think the matter over. Another C.O. asked, "How can we think it over when President Wilson is doing all the thinking for us?" The colonel stared through him and left.

The following afternoon, Colonel Waterman returned and asked us our decision. We refused as a body. The colonel then proceeded to order eight men, previously selected, one by one, to shovel a pile of refuse outside the

Conscientious objectors (front) William Dunham, Howard Moore, Henry Monsky, Sam Solnitski, (back) Evan Thomas, Harold Gray, Roderick Seidenburg at the Fort Riley, Kansas, tent camp, 1918. Photo courtesy of Swarthmore College Peace Collection.

kitchen into a wagon. They refused, were placed under arrest, and marched off to the guardhouse.

The rest of us were told that we could not leave the camp, and we noticed that there were guards stationed all around to see that we obeyed the order.

The next day, Wednesday, September 18th, the colonel returned and repeated the procedure. Eight more men were ordered to shovel the same pile of refuse. Seven of them refused in turn. The eighth man shoveled for a while. Colonel Waterman ordered the lieutenant to send this man to the barracks, because he was willing to work.

At that point I was startled to hear my name called out. The colonel ordered me to shovel some cans. I told him that I would do my share but that I could not do it for the other men. When I did not move, the colonel asked me again. I told him that I would do my share. After going through this several times, the colonel realized that I meant by my share that I was joining the other men in not shoveling the pile of refuse. I was placed under arrest.

We were told to pack our things. A guard party surrounded us. The lieutenant marched us to the guardhouse, and although most of the men were loaded down with baggage, he would not let us stop to rest. After several minutes, Joseph Brandon yelled out, "Halt!" The guards were compelled to stop with us. We could see that the lieutenant was annoyed that one of the C.O.s had taken away his command. Several minutes later, someone else called "Halt!" We stopped. The lieutenant said nothing.

On Thursday, 51 more men received the same command to clean up the rubbish. All but seven refused to obey the colonel's order. The following week the remaining C.O.s were given rakes and were ordered to clean up the entire camp. Of the 30 in the tent colony, 27 refused.

Chapter Six

My Sincerity Is Judged

We were placed in solitary. The cell that I occupied was about four feet wide, six feet long, and eight feet high. The only windows were upstairs in the cell block. Very little light and fresh air seeped down to us.

The bed was a sheet of steel, which raised against the wall. I seldom raised it because there was nothing else to sit on. The toilet facilities were in another section of the cell block, and when I wanted to relieve myself, I had to attract the attention of a guard who would then escort me there.

Lieutenant Pike, who was in charge of the guardhouse, asked us to go out to work. When we refused, he told us that we would only get bread and water. After eating bread and drinking water for several days, some of us stopped eating altogether. The lieutenant gave in, and we were fed and placed in a large cage with some of the other objectors.

On June 1, 1918, Mr. Baker, Secretary of War, appointed a Board of Inquiry to determine the sincerity of conscientious objectors who had declined to accept noncombatant service or had not been assigned because they were considered insincere by their camp commanders. How they, or anyone else, can measure the sincerity of another person I cannot understand. But in the army, there are many actions being done that no person with common sense can understand.

During the last week of September, the Board of Inquiry arrived at Fort Riley. This board consisted of Major Walter G. Kellogg of the Judge Advocate General's department; Julian W. Mack, Judge of the United States Circuit Court of Appeals; and Harlan F. Stone of the Columbia Law School.

Lieutenant Pike had marched us to the post headquarters, but we found that the Board was occupied with the men left in the tent colony. On the way back, the lieutenant insisted on using military commands in conducting the "march." He was furious when we did not follow his orders. He ordered his men to close us up when we walked along leisurely. One of the guards struck Caplowitz twice in the back with the butt of his gun. Caplowitz fell and two of us had to carry him. Lieutenant Pike continued his bullying tactics by pushing another objector, calling him a "god-damned bastard" while doing it.

Back in the guardhouse, Joseph Brandon drew up a letter to Colonel Waterman telling him of Lieutenant Pike's behavior. Somehow, news of the letter leaked out to Pike, who came down to our cell and asked us if we had not been treated properly. The boys let out a thunderous "No!"

"Bread and water!" he replied and left.

The next morning Brandon gave Pike the letter at breakfast — a breakfast of bread and water. Pike sneered at us for not eating. When we arrived downstairs, Pike sent Branden back to solitary.

In mid-morning, we were marched again to post headquarters for our interviews to determine our "sincerity."

We were brought into a large room of one of the army barracks where the three interviewers were seated in different sections of the room about 50 feet away from one another so as not to be disturbed. They divided the men up. I was being questioned by Judge Mack, who was the chairman of the Board.

I do not remember the exact questions and answers of the interview, but it went something like this:

Question: Your name? **Answer:** Max Sandin.

Q. Are you a citizen of this country?

A. Yes.

Q. From which county did you come?

A. Russia.

Q. Why did you leave Russia?

A. I didn't want to serve in the army.

Q. Why did you come to the United States?

A. Because it is a free country, and there is enough work for everybody who is able and willing to work.

Q. What were you doing in Russia for a living?

A. I was a shoemaker.

Q. How much did you earn a week?

A. Two rubles.

Q. How did you live?

A. Very poor.

Q. Did you eat meat every day?

A. No. Maybe two days a week.

Q. Do you eat meat every day in this country?

A. Yes.

Q. How many suits of clothes did you have in Russia?

A. One suit.

Q. How many suits do you have here?

A. Three suits.

Q. How many pairs of shoes did you have in Russia?

A. One pair.

Q. And here?

A. Three pair.

Q. Are your mother and father living?

A. Yes.

Q. How many rooms did you live in?

A. One room.

Q. Do you have sisters or brothers?

A. I have two brothers and one sister.

Q. Did you all live in one room?

A. Yes.

Q. How did you manage to sleep there?

A. It is impossible to explain.

Q. And how many rooms do you have here?

A. I own a two-family house, five rooms for each family — with a partner.

Q. What else do you have here that you did not have in Russia?

A. I have a high school education and a new Ford.

"Now, according to your own statement, which you made voluntarily, you came here as a poor immigrant, and this country welcomed you and gave you an opportunity to have all the good things. Tell me why do you refuse to be thankful to this country and fight to protect all these good things?

I told him that I was morally opposed to killing, although not because the bible says "Thou shalt not kill." I pointed to the many governments and religious hypocrites who preach that the bible is a holy God-given book, but who put it aside to kill when it comes to war.

"No, I will not kill my fellow men even if you, meaning this government, will kill me. I will die some time anyway. I would rather die a free man rather than kill or be killed like a dog."

"Look through the window," I told the interviewer. "You see all those buildings, the paved streets, the crops, the orchards, the cars, all these things? We, as workers, built them. I, as a worker, did my share. Nobody gave me something for nothing, so I do not have to be thankful to anybody. If the United States government believes that I am not entitled to have all these goods, for which I worked, they may take everything I have and send me out of the country.

"When I became a citizen in 1916, I took an oath to protect the Constitution with my life. I am ready and willing to do that now as in 1916. But I want to remind you that Article 13 (Slavery) Section I (Abolition) of the Constitution states: 'Neither slavery nor involuntary servitude, except as a punishment for crime whereas the party shall have been duly convicted, shall exist within the United States, or any place subject to their jurisdiction.'

At the end of the hearing, Judge Mack said, off the record, "You men are right, but you are 200 years ahead of your time."

"And what crime did I commit for which I have to serve forcibly in the army?"

At the end of the hearing, Judge Mack said, off the record, "You men are right, but you are 200 years ahead of your time." [ED. NOTE: *Another 100 years to go!*]

I was judged sincere by the Board of Inquiry.

CHAPTER SEVEN

Reign of Terror

[EDITOR'S NOTE: *From September 5th to October 21st, C.O.s were systematically tortured by the officers and guards at Camp Funston. They were kicked, shoved, beaten with rifles, prodded with bayonets while being forced to exercise, dragged on the ground if they refused to march in formation, choked, awakened at all hours and forced out into the cold, thrown into cold showers multiple times a day and scrubbed with toilet brushes, refused food, held in unsanitary conditions, and more. Multiple requests to appeal to a higher authority were refused — or the higher authority sanctioned the treatment. They also faced verbal taunts and extreme prejudice by other prisoners and guards alike as many were Jewish or immigrants, including others from Russia like Max.*]

On September 27th, I was transferred with seven others to the guardhouse at Camp Funston, which was adjacent to Fort Riley. We joined the seven who had been tortured in the Fort Riley guardhouse, and in the ensuing weeks we were joined by others from Fort Riley.

A diary[6] of those tortures was read on the floor of the House of Representatives by William E. Mason of Illinois on March 3, 1919. The following quotations are from that diary:

Friday, September 27. Again, while exercising, the men were grossly maltreated. The bayonet was applied to all of us. Larsen receiving a scar. Kaplan and Breger were beaten with the butt end of the rifle. All were kicked and shoved about.

---

[6] *"Report of Treatment of Conscientious Objectors at the Camp Funston Guard House"; see Appendix 1 for the more complete diary and letter signed by the tortured C.O.s*

Eight conscientious objectors came here from the Fort Riley guardhouse. [Max: "I was one of them."]

After supper we were ordered outside where we formed in double rank. The sergeant of the guards issued some military commands to us. When we did not obey promptly, he shoved us about violently. We then began marching around the building. Orders were given to "double time." Bayonets were pressed against the bodies of Larsen, Silver, and others to obtain compliance, but no one ran. The guards now insisted that we walk in strict military posture and cuffs, kicks, and blows were rained upon those who failed to do so. Eichel refused to submit to this abuse and informed the guard that since in his opinion exercise was optional with conscientious objectors, he would march no more under such brutal impositions. A guard seized him by the neck and forced him around the building, heaping blows and kicks upon him at the same time. When he was finally released, the back of his head was covered with bumps and he was sore all over.

At about 9 that evening we were again ordered out and again put through the same ordeal. This time Steiner ceased walking. He was seized by the ears and dragged around the building. Another guard after a while seized him by the throat and choked him so forcibly that he sank breathless to the ground. Steiner reported his treatment to the officer of the day, a second lieutenant, who refused to give his name and insisted that he was carrying out orders.

We were informed that we would be called out every two hours. At 11 p.m. we were awakened and ordered out. We refused. It was debated whether or not to forcibly drag us out. They finally decided to leave us alone. However, none could sleep, for the thought that we might be roused any moment kept preying upon our minds.

Saturday, September 28. At 8:30 p.m. the sergeant of the guards ordered us out. Expecting a repetition of yesterday's affair, especially so since the sergeant was a veritable brute, we refused. Kaplan, half undressed, was the first to rouse his venom. He was lifted bodily off his bed and thrown against the bedstead so forcibly that his skull might have been smashed. He was then ordered to put on his shoes. He refused. The sergeant seized him and put him out barefooted. The other men were similarly handled. When we were finally lined up outside, the sergeant following us out — and never did man gloat so over his accomplishment — he remarked that he was carrying out the major's orders, meaning Major Taussig, the military police officer. After marching around a while, we were permitted to return to quarters. Threats of subsequent and periodic repetition of this treatment again had the effect of keeping us awake and expectant all night.

The instructions that conscientious objectors are to be permitted to exercise are being utilized as a means to impose hardships upon us. We are kept outdoors in all sorts of weather, from six to eight hours each day, and the guards are instructed to see to it that we keep moving continually. This is a source of constant irritation and friction between us and the guards, for some of us find it physically impossible to keep walking all day.

Our correspondence privilege has been restricted to one letter a week. The letter must be written upon one side of one small sheet. Its contents are subjected to careful censorship.

A general and thorough raid was made upon our quarters for books, magazines, and other reading matter.

All prisoners were ordered to take a cold shower.

Sunday, October 6. In the afternoon, Sandin collapsed while taking his second cold shower of the day. We explained to the doctor who called, the nature of the treatment we had been receiving lately. We also informed him that we were being underfed.

The captain, who was "officer of the day," ordered that we be deprived of supper because we did not stand at "attention" at roll-call.

At midnight we were suddenly and unexpectedly roused by the sergeant of the guards and ordered to take a cold shower. It was obvious that this was an unreasonable and vicious imposition and most of us refused to get up. We were then violently dragged into the shower room and held underneath the spray, night clothes and all, until thoroughly exhausted. Kaplan, Breger, Block, Powell, Franklin, Eichel, Downey, Steiner, and Da Rosa were so treated. The "officer of the day" was present and directed the proceedings.

Monday, October 7. Greenberg, Block, Bernstein, and others have gone on sick report this morning, suffering from colds. Block and Bernstein were given aspirin tablets to make them perspire. Though the day was rainy and damp, all hands were ordered out for exercise. We were kept outside in the drizzle, until ordered to come in for a cold shower. Even those who have taken aspirin tablets were not excused from the prescribed bath.

Breger, Monsky, Ott, Silver, Da Rosa, Block, and Eichel have already declared an absolute hunger-strike as a vehement protest against this treatment.

Tuesday, October 8. Franklin, Sandin, and Hennessey have joined the hunger strike as protest against our inhuman treatment.

At about 8 p.m. the order was issued to prepare for a cold shower. Monsky informed the captain, who directed proceedings, that he would not undress. The captain ordered a guard to undress and keep him under the shower twice as long. The sergeant of the guards timed everyone. Monsky was kept under the spray an unusually long time. He finally heard the captain say, "If he suffers, keep him there; but if he isn't suffering let him go."

Franklin, because of his collapse the previous evening, was given an extra dose and again collapsed. Eichel again requested to be permitted to see the post commander and again was refused.

Quite a few of the men, thoroughly chilled by the shower, had gone to bed to warm up. "Attention" was suddenly called and those in bed were dumped by the guards and dragged to their feet, half naked. The guards proceeded to place them in military posture. Towels, socks, and ropes were utilized to tie their hands in proper position. Then the captain addressed us. "How many of you will now become sensible objectors and go out to do some work this afternoon?" Receiving no favorable response, he said tersely: "All right, another cold shower at 10:30 a.m."

We were then ordered to dress and go out for exercise. Quite a few refusing to do this were rudely dressed and dragged outside.

Friday, October 11. Brandon, because of extreme weakness, was unable to walk. A guard pricked him with a bayonet, and then the sergeant of the guards pushed him around.

Saturday, October 12. In the afternoon all the men, regardless of their physical condition, were ordered to dress and go out for fresh air. Those who refused were forcibly dressed and thrust outside. The men, because of their weakened state, sprawled all over the ground while groups of the spectators watched the miserable and sorry sight.

At various times during the afternoon Block, Breger, and Silver collapsed from total exhaustion.

After supper the men were taken out of the solitary cells and returned to the regular squad room.

Monday, October 14. Major Taussig, accompanied by another major, who introduced himself as our investigator, came into the room in the morning. The latter gazed sneeringly and insolently about the room and without much ado dismissed most of the men from his mind as "Russian foreigners." His questioning was confined for the most part to ascertaining the birth and nativity of the men and establishing them as "Pro-Germans and members of Von Ludendorff's third division." He finally asked, with studied irony, whether any man was in danger of losing his reason or even his life. His final remark was, "There isn't a single American in the crowd."

Our writing tablets and what little money was in our possession were taken from us. A special guard was placed over us.

Tuesday, October 15. Silver was examined by the doctor, and it was apparent that his condition was very poor. He was hardly able to get out of bed. In the afternoon, he was taken out of our guard room and placed in a solitary cell.

Monday, October 21. The major who made the perfunctory investigation Monday, October 14, returned and began calling each man to explain the mistreatments he had experienced and witnessed.

We wish it known that during this tense period we were held absolutely incommunicado. Packages containing food and delicacies, sent us from home at a great expense of time, money, and sentiment, were viciously and wantonly destroyed and their contents dumped in the garbage cans, though we had at no time been told that we could not receive such packages.

The above is only a brief summary of the atrocities perpetrated upon us. The situation can never be described with sufficient vividness and intensity to impart to the authorities a real impression of the mental and physical anguish suffered by us. Most of the mistreatments took place outside, with large groups watching the sorry and revolting spectacle of defenseless men being most brutally punched, shoved, and abused.

While we do not wish to impugn the motives of the investigator, we have reason to believe, because of his own statements and his obviously antagonistic attitude, that the report of his investigation would be prejudiced and not strictly in accordance with the fullest testimony of the men. We therefore feel justified in submitting this report, which we are willing to affirm under oath, merely as a confirmation to his report.

The men reached the Guard House at Funston on the follow dates — and went through the above experiences from the day of their arrival.

September 8th.

Bernstein, Breger, Greenberg, Kaplan, Henessey, Larsen, Powell.

September 27.

Downey, Eichel, Franklin, Ott, Sandin, Shotkin, Silver, Steiner.

September 30.

Block, Da Rosa, Monsky.

October 8.

Brandon

A copy of this report has been given to the investigator.

We the undersigned, consider the above a fair and accurate account of our treatment at the military police guardhouse of Camp Funston, Kansas.

Morris Franklin, Thomas Shotkin, Herman Kaplan, Lester G. Ott, Joseph Brandon, Ulysses Da Rosa, Mayer Bernstein, Henry Monsky, Max Sandin, Emanuel Silver, Benjamin Breger, Rexford Powell, David Eichel, Julius R. Greenberg, Charles P. Larsen, Francis Steiner, Francis X. Henessey, and John Downey

I received the following telegram from my sister on October 20th:

Max Sandin, Military Police Guard house, Funston Kansas.

"How are you? Why don't you write? Answer prepaid." – Sarah Glass

CHAPTER EIGHT

Sentenced To Be Shot

On October 21, 1918, Downey, Shotkin, Steiner, Silver, Brandon, and I were escorted to the Judge Advocate's office where we learned that a court martial was waiting for us. When I arrived with three guards (one on each side of me and one behind) armed with rifles and fixed bayonets, an officer gave them orders, "Shoot to kill if he tries to run away." This was the first time that the army had seen fit to tell us that we were to be tried.

The Judge Advocate told us that we were being charged with violating Article 64 of the army's rules and regulations for refusing to clean up that pile of rubbish at Fort Riley.

I remembered the lieutenant at Camp Gordon who had given me a copy of the articles and had told me to note Article 64: "In time of war when a private strikes or disobeys his superior officer, he shall be court-martialed, and may be punishable by death."

I did not expect to receive any justice. I could taste the blood in my mouth from the time that my teacher had slapped me in *cheder* for questioning God's words. I remembered my poor brother Gabriel who had been killed in the Russo-Japanese War. Would I be next?

When we came into the large military barrack, there were 13 army officers (mostly majors and captains) with their sidearms sitting around a big wooden table. I stood there unshaven and wearing a pair of gray size-42 pants tied with a clothesline because my regular pant size was 34. One of the officers said, "Private Max Sandin, this is your court-martial." I replied, "I am not in the army and I do not recognize you." They started to ask me questions but I did not answer except for one question. I answered "yes" to "Do you want a copy of these proceedings?"

I did not answer when asked if I had a lawyer. So, the assistant provost marshal was appointed to defend me. The reason I did not defend myself was that I knew whatever I said would be no good. They were not here to try me. They were here to condemn me. I did not expect justice from a militaristic government that sends its young boys, who never committed a crime, to the slaughterhouse. What could I tell them?

> The court then proceeded to the trial of Max Sandin, Private, Company A, First Casual Battalion, Conscientious Objectors, Fort Riley, Kansas, who does not desire counsel.[7]
>
> **The Judge Advocate:** In compliance with Section 96, M.C.M., 1917, I desire to state to the court that the Judge Advocate has advised the accused as follows: that he has the right to have counsel; that if he does not desire counsel it will be the duty of the Judge Advocate to act as his counsel; the nature of the charges and specifications against him; that he has a right to have a copy of the record of the trial; the nature of the evidence against him; that a plea of not guilty is not a denial of guilt but merely a refusal to admit guilt and a demand upon the prosecution to prove the charges; that the maximum penalty that may be imposed upon each of the specifications if found guilty is death; that he has a right to offer any evidence and testimony he may desire; that he may testify in his own behalf subject to cross

---

[7] *Editors' note: The proceedings quoted are from the official transcript with ellipses used to eliminate irrelevant material.*

examination; and also may make a statement to the court, verbal or written, not under oath; and that any evidence he may desire to call will be summoned before the court.

Is that correct (The Accused: Yes sir.) [I did not answer as the record indicated I did.]

…

The accused was then arraigned upon the following charge and specification, which were read by the Judge Advocate.

Charge 1: Violation of the 64th Article of War.

Specification 1: In that Private Max Sandin, Company A, First Casual Battalion, Conscientious Objectors, having received a lawful command from Colonel J. G. Waterman, his superior officer, to clean up a pile of refuse and dirt in his camp, on or about the 18th of September, willfully disobeyed the same. William E. Donaldson, First Lieutenant Infantry.

…

(The following is the testimony of Colonel J. G. Waterman who was examined by the Assistant Judge Advocate)

Q. State your full name, rank, organization and station.

A. J. C. Waterman, Colonel Cavalry, Fort Riley, Kansas.

Q. Do you know the accused? If so, state who he is.

A. I know him as Max Sandin, Private of Company A, First Casual Battalion, a conscientious objector.

Q. Colonel, have you ever had any reason to note the accused before? If so, will you kindly state about whom and where it happened and what the occasion was?

A. More than once. On one occasion, the 18th of September, 1918, at the Casual Camp in Fort Riley, Kansas, I had occasion there to give him an order to load some refuse near the kitchen into a wagon. Do you want me to go on?

Q. Please, sir, tell what happened?

A. He said "I can't conscientiously do it." He says, "I can do my share but I can't for these other men." I told him to go ahead and clean up the pile of refuse, that that was his share just now, to do what I told him to do. He said he couldn't do it, refused to do it, and I asked him if he refused to do as I told him to do. He absolutely refused to obey the order to load that dirt in the wagon. He said he refused. I told him to step aside and had him confined and charges preferred against him.

Q. Did he do any of this work?

A. No, he did not.

Q. Colonel, have you ever explained noncombatant service to this man?

A. Yes sir, on September 17th, 1918, it was on that date I think, I explained it to all of these objectors in camp at Fort Riley there. I read it to them and explained to them as well as I was able — it was in plain words and didn't need much explaining — then I went up to each one of the men, of which the accused was one, and asked if they understood. They all said they did. I stepped them out and said "Those that desire noncombatant service in either of these three branches as just read, step out to the front." Nobody stepped out. This accused did not step out, would not accept it.

Q. Do you know for a fact that this accused was present at the time?

A. I believe he was, yes sir. I saw so many of them it is a little difficult to say, but I think you have better witnesses than I. However, I am firmly of the opinion that he was present at the time.

The accused was at the time given opportunity to cross examine the witness but stood mute and declined.

No examination by the court.

Lt. Donaldson, First Lieutenant, Infantry, U.S. Army, Commanding Company A, First Casual Battalion, Conscientious Objectors, Fort Riley, Kansas, a witness for the prosecution, was sworn and testified as follows:

Direct Examination by the Prosecution:

Q. State your full name rank, organization and station.

A. William E. Donaldson, First Lieutenant, Infantry, U.S. Army, Commanding Company A, First Casual Battalion, Conscientious Objectors, Fort Riley, Kansas

Q. Do you know the accused? If so, state who he is.

A. Private Max Sandin, Company A, First Casual Battalion, Conscientious Objectors, Fort Riley, Kansas

Q. Have you ever had any reason to note the accused before? If so, state about when and where it happened and the occasion.

A. I was present in the camp of Company A, First Casual Battalion, Conscientious Objectors, on or about September 18, 1918, and I heard Colonel Waterman, Commanding Officer, Fort Riley, Kansas, order Pvt. Max Sandin to clean up a pile of dirt and refuse in this camp. Pvt. Max Sandin replied "I cannot conscientiously do it but will volunteer to do my share, but I cannot do it for the other men in camp." Colonel Waterman then told him that he would have to do what he was told to do and again ordered him to start to work. Private Max Sandin replied, "I tell you no." Colonel Waterman then said to him, "You refuse to do this, work? You refuse to do what I tell you?" Private Sandin replied, "Yes I refuse."

Q. Did he do it?

A. No sir.

Q. Lieutenant, do you know whether or not the President's Executive Order was ever explained to this man?

A. Yes sir, on two occasions, September 17th, 1918, and September 18th, 1918.

Q. Was this man present?'

A. I saw him standing in the group of men when the order was being read by the colonel.

Q. What order was that that was explained to them?

A. The President's Executive Order, C.C. 28, in regard to non-combatant service in the Quartermaster Corps, in the Engineer's Corps or the Medical Corps and its different branches,

Q. Did this man accept such service?

A. No sir.

Q. Do you know whether or not this man has ever accepted any pay from the Government?

A. This man has not accepted any but he has insurance for $10,000.00 and he also has a Class F Allotment of $15.00 a month.

The accused was given opportunity to cross examine witness, but again stood mute and declined.

Examination by the Court:

Q. What religion does this man belong to?

A. I believe the man is an atheist.

Q. You don't know on what ground this man's objections are on?

A. Atheists don't believe in God, Christ, Churches and so on.

Q. Do you know what grounds he conscientiously objects to?

A. I believe — as far as I know it is religious grounds, based on readings he has read in the bible.

Q. I thought you said he was an atheist. I wanted to know whether it was religious grounds.

A. I believe it is religious grounds.

Q. You don't know whether he belongs to any sect?

A. He doesn't belong to any sect to my knowledge. He is a Russian Jew.

THE PRESIDENT: You the accused are informed that you have the right to testify in your own behalf, and subject to cross examination offer any evidence in denial, in explanation, or in contradiction of the charge against you. If you do testify your testimony will be given the weight of evidence the same as any other witness, and you may not be cross examined beyond the field of your direct examination, except to test your credibility as a witness. You may also make an unsworn verbal or written statement of the case, with such explanation of allegation of motive, excuse, matter of extenuation, etc., as you may desire to offer, or it may embrace with the facts, a presentation also of the law of the case and an argument both upon the facts and the law. Such statement is not testimony and therefore is not subject to cross-examination, but as a personal defense or argument, however, it may and properly should be taken into consideration by the court. You do not have to do either and your failure to do either will not create any presumptions against you. Do you fully understand all that I have said to you? (The accused stands mute and refuses to answer.) Knowing these rights, do you now wish to testify or to make a statement in your own behalf or to do either? (The accused stands mute and refuses to answer.)

The Assistant Judge Advocate: I would like to ask the court to take into consideration the absolute surly, indifference of the accused in this case, branding him as one who has no respect for law of any kind or any order and I ask that the court pass the extreme penalty of the law for disobedience of this order.

The accused was given an opportunity to make a statement in his own behalf, but he stood mute and refused.

— Charles L. Brewster, Major, Infantry, 164th D.B.,

President George Imbrie, 2nd Lt. Infantry, Trial Judge Advocate.

After all the testimony against me was presented and I did not answer, the assistant provost marshal — my court-appointed defense counsel — spoke on my behalf, pointing his finger at me and saying, "I would like to ask the court to take into consideration the absolute surly indifference of the accused in this case, branding him as one who has no respect for law of any kind or any order, and I ask that the court pass the extreme penalty of the law for disobedience of this order." And the court was not stingy. The whole court-martial took about 30 minutes. But these 30 minutes were the best in my 28 years of life at that time.

The conscientious objector court-martialed after me was Lester Ott, a lawyer from Hamilton, Ohio. When I came out of the courtroom, he took the record of my proceedings and made notes. When he was called in, he acted as his own counsel. His trial took four hours and the results were the same.

The court-martial did not tell me what my sentence was but I quickly found out from the guards that I had been sentenced to be shot.

That evening, after supper, we were searched as we left the dining hall to see that we did not have any knives or forks on us. They weren't very thorough, however, because they had left us our razors.

Ten of us were sentenced to death that day for refusing to clean up a pile of rubbish. I suppose we were to be made examples of so that men would be frightened into obeying any commands given them, including murder.

And now our lives were to be snuffed out, because we had refused to give up our humanity.

Frequently Asked Questions

Many people have asked me questions about how I felt at that moment. They are really interested and would like to have answers from a person who had the honor, privilege, and courage to live through it.

Did I know that the court-martial could sentence me to be shot?
Yes, I knew. In the guardhouse, they gave me a little booklet with the rules of the army. One of the rules (Article 64) was, "If a soldier in time of war refuses an order of his superior officer, he, the soldier, is punishable by death." I could not expect more than death.

How did I feel at that moment?
I felt that this moment is the hallow of humanity and I was glad to be one of the lucky men to receive this honor.

What were you thinking that moment when you faced those 13 men with whom your life was given to their caprice?
I was thinking about Spinoza, Jesus before he became the son of a god, of the five Haymarket martyrs, Sacco and Vanzetti, Hirsh Lekert of Vilnius, Rosa Luxemburg and Karl Liebknecht of Germany, and of all those who were hanged or shot by the ruling class.

Did they tell you at the end of the court-martial what the sentence was?
No, they did not tell me. But after the court-martial, all the ten conscientious objectors were put in one cell at Fort Riley guardhouse. The dining room was upstairs and every day, after every meal, we were searched going downstairs. They were looking for knives and forks hidden in pockets so as not to commit suicide. But at the same time, we had our razors. And the prisoners sentenced to a number of years were sent to Fort Leavenworth.

Chapter Nine

Waiting . . .

The day and night after my court-martial were long ones. Downey was told to pack his belongings on November 1st. Shotkin, Monsky, and Silver were transferred from the Camp Funston guardhouse on November 2nd. Austria surrendered on the fifth. On the morning of the eleventh, we were awakened by whistles from Junction City. At last, Germany had surrendered.

We did not expect to be executed now that the war was over, but our experience with military justice made us contain our joy.

Word of the reign of terror in the Camp Funston guardhouse had reached the outside world. The War Department sent Brigadier General Williams to interview us. We were happily surprised to be addressed by him as "Mr." The other prisoners, we learned later, had corroborated our testimony. The treatment that we had received had turned their scorn for us "slackers" into respect.

On November 27th, Kaplan, Steiner, Breger, Ott, Schneider, Bernstein, Brandon, Greenberg, and I were told to pack our belongings. We were handcuffed to one another and placed in a truck. We thought that we were being transferred to the Disciplinary Barracks at Fort Leavenworth, but, to our surprise, we were taken back to the guardhouse at Fort Riley. There to greet us was our old friend Lieutenant Pike, who grinned menacingly at us.

Lieutenant Pike grabbed our belongings and ordered us downstairs where he had us placed in solitary. Greenberg asked an officer why we were not placed in a large cage with the other objectors. The officer said because we were to be shot.

Fortunately for us, however, these sentences could not be executed until President Wilson, who was in Europe, had reviewed them. This ruling had been made after several soldiers who had been involved in a race riot in Texas had been court-martialed and hanged immediately afterwards. These men had been Negroes, and this lynching had stirred up quite a bit of public protest.*

Meanwhile, we had to wait in the death cells of Fort Riley guardhouse for 14 weeks until Wilson's return.

The days dragged on, and the harassment of the officers and guards could be counted on as much as the sun rising every morning. We were not permitted anything to read, but the prisoners who went out to work used to sneak us reading and writing material, cigarettes, candy, and other such items.

Thanksgiving Day we had turkey and all the trimmings that go with it, including at least five different kinds of pie. But it was not like Thanksgiving at home.

One beautiful Indian-summer day, I noticed a guard walk past my cell several times. Finally, he stopped and said: "Mister, I envy you and am jealous that you are on the inside and I am on the outside watching you. I too am a member of the Socialist Party, but I did not have the courage to take a stand as you had. In the barracks they say you will get twenty-five years in prison. Really, I don't know what to do."

I advised him to say no and then his worries would be over too. I pointed to the next two cells, which were empty, and said that he could reserve the best.

He asked me what he could do for me.

I asked for something to read.

Several weeks passed by, but my friend did not return. One morning another

---

*Houston race riot of 1917, also known as the Camp Logan Mutiny

guard stopped at my cell and gave me a package. Inside were two copies of *Die Zukunft*, a Socialist monthly, the *Nation*, envelopes, writing paper, stamps, pencils, and cigarettes. I gave the cigarettes to my cell neighbors because I have never smoked. We all enjoyed the magazines and other material.

I never saw this guard again or the one who had sent the bundle. I hope that these unknown soldiers are not in unknown graves.

One afternoon I was reading a story about a Russian revolutionist who ran away from Siberia. I became so engrossed in the story that I forgot about the checkup. A guard called "Attention!" It was too late to get up, so I hid the magazines in the open toilet and remained on the floor where I had been reading "No supper tonight!" the officer of the day ordered, seeing me on the floor.

The other prisoners did not know what was going on, but when they heard the officer, they too refused to get up. He repeated the order in each cell to no avail. By this time, we were used to not eating, or just getting bread and water.

Another time, I was sitting on the toilet when a guard and a new officer of the day came in. I did not get up when the guard commanded "Attention!" The officer of the day wanted to know why I remained seated. The guard explained that I was a C.O.

"What, a commanding officer?"

"No, a conscientious objector."

"To hell with him then," the officer said and walked out.

Among the things we lacked most in the Fort Riley guardhouse were fresh air and exercise. Very little light and fresh air seeped down to our cells from the windows in the cell block on the floor above.

One morning, a group of us cooked up a scheme and decided to report for sick call. Our cell doors were opened and the guards marched us out into that wonderful fresh air and sunshine for the first time in weeks, for a ten-minute walk to the infirmary.

When we arrived at the infirmary, the doctor asked us what was the matter. We told him that we needed fresh air and exercise and that we hadn't had any for weeks.

"You'll get plenty of it if you'll go out to work with the other prisoners," the doctor scolded.

One of the boys said, "What about that Hippocrates oath you took, doctor?"

The next morning, we went on sick call again and gave the doctor the same reason. This time the army retaliated by withholding our breakfast, but the fresh air was worth it.

This went on for several days until finally the army found a way to keep us from getting fresh air and sunshine. The doctor came to us in the guardhouse.

One evening, while we were in the large cage, one of the C.O.s had to relieve himself. He rattled a drinking cup on the iron grating to attract the attention of a guard. The officer of the day was new and apparently did not like us or the rattling, so he gave an order to the guards that none of us was to be let out of the cage until the changing of the guard the next morning.

When we heard his order, we all started rattling tin cups on the grating, but the guards paid no attention to us. Eventually, the officer of the day came back and ordered us to stop the noise. We told him that we would stop if he would let us use the toilet. The officer refused to budge from his earlier command, so we continued the rattling. He called the riot squad, and in a few minutes the cell block was packed with soldiers with rifles and fixed bayonets.

The prison officer arrived on the scene. He listened to our complaint and the officer's story. He told the officer of the day that he had done the right thing. Upon hearing this, we unfastened our trousers and defecated on the floor. The astonished prison officer placed us in solitary.

The next day, we were moved back into the cage, which, thanks to the guards, was cleaner than ever. From that moment on, the guards let us out whenever we called them.

CHAPTER TEN

Death by Inches

The story of military tortures and brutalities slowly leaked out to the world. This was not easy because all our mail was censored. But the prisoners who went to work posted letters for us. We did not know what sort of reaction the outside world would have to them, because war always makes people irrational and cruel. As was to be expected, the newspapers remained silent.

Gradually, however, increasing pressure on the War Department by individuals and such groups as the National Civil Liberties Bureau (the early name of the American Civil Liberties Union), brought about some changes. On December 6th, the manacling of prisoners to cell doors was abandoned. The following story was released by the War Department News Bureau on that day:

The Secretary of War authorized the following statement:

Disciplinary regulations in force in military prisons have been modified by the War Department Order. Fastening of prisoners to the bars of cells will no more be used as a mode of punishment. This and milder devices have been effective in the past in breaking the willful or stubborn opposition of prisoners of the usual military type, who would not submit to the work requirements of disciplinary barracks. Instead of being allowed to lie in bunks while others worked, they have been compelled to choose between working or standing in discomfort during working hours. Practically, under usual conditions, this has been more a threat than an actuality, and as such it has been effective. But during recent months, with the influx of political prisoners to disciplinary barracks, particularly at Fort Leavenworth, extremity of attitude on the part of this new type of prisoner has at times led to extremity of discipline as provided by military regulations. These clearly were not formulated with the political type of prisoner in mind, and their effectiveness as deterrents has been questionable. Men have returned for repeated experiences of the severest forms of discipline. The most extreme of these is now discarded and the order is comprehensive. It applies not merely to political prisoners, but to those of every type.

The following are excerpts from a statement of conditions at Fort Jay on August 20th, as reported by Dr. Judah Magnes and John S. Codman, for the National Civil Liberties Bureau, and which was later included in the remarks of William Mason on the floor of the House of Representatives:

The door of Sterenstein's cell was opened first. We found him with his wrists shackled to the iron bars of the small opening in the door. He was in his underwear and in bare feet. There was no pail in his cell. The only thing in the cell was a blanket. When Julius Eichel's (the brother of David Eichel who was with me in Camp Funston) cell was opened we found him shackled in the same way to the bars of the grating in the door. He was in his underclothes and had on one stocking. There was a pail in his cell.

Maj. Ward explained to us that they were sentenced to solitary confinement for refusing to work and obey prison instructions.... They were shackled to the bars of the grating from 7:30 a.m. to 11:00 a.m. and then from 12:00 p.m. to 4:30 p.m. — the theory being that this is equivalent to an eight-hour working day. They are given two slices of bread three times a day and a pitcher of water three times a day. They are given no water with which to wash. If they wish to wash, they must use some of their drinking water. They are not permitted a toothbrush.

They are taken on Saturday night and given a shower bath.

After 14 days of such confinement the prisoners are released into the prison yard for 14 days. They are given raw food, an ax for chopping wood, cooking utensils, and shelter at night. Otherwise, they are regarded as men on a desert island, bound to shift for themselves. If after these 14 days of desert island life, they are still unwilling to yield their conscientious convictions, they are placed in solitary confinement again for another 14 days. This can go on indefinitely for the term of 20 or 30 years to which these men have been sentenced or until they are broken, either physically or mentally.

Of those who suffered most from military brutalities in the prison camps were the Molokans, a religious sect which had come to this country from Russia on the understanding that they would not have to serve in the armed forces. On registration day, thirty-four Molokans held religious services in front of the draft board in Glendale, Arizona. After the services, they went inside and informed the chairman that they would not register for the draft. These thirty-four wound up in civil prisons and six of them eventually in military prisons.

On August 2, 1918, an officer came up to these six at Fort Huachuca, Arizona, and said "You must become soldiers." When the Molokans answered that they would not, the officer said "We will force you to." The Molokans replied "Force is with you."

Ivan Sussoff explains in a letter to his wife what happened next:

The next day as usual the horn blew to go out to drill. We did not go out. Suddenly the officer with a few others rushed in and roughly ordered us to go out to drill. We said we would not go because our religion forbids it. After a long argument the officer left us and we went to prepare our breakfasts. After breakfast they did not let us go back. They took us over to the soldiers who were ordered by the officers to force us to drill. Every four soldiers took a hold of every one of us. First, they took F.V.K. and put him in the row, but he would not stand in the row. Then they took me in the same way and as I resisted, they took me on their arms and put me in the row. I lifted my arms to God and prayed him to help me, and then I fell to the ground. They lifted

"Force is with you."

up again. There were more than four hundred soldiers and also many officers. I told them: "Listen citizens! If you want to do something to us, do it right here. Don't torture us." And I prayed to God again. Then they took Noisy the same way. He also resisted, fell on the ground and prayed. Then they did the same with Fedor, who fell on the ground as a dead man, and the same they did with Jacob.

The officer ordered them to lift us up, but the soldiers could not. Then the officer sent for the colonel. The colonel came soon and asked which of us spoke English best. They pointed at Kulikov, who was lying near me. When Kulikov was ordered to get up, he did not move, and the colonel ordered us to lift him up. "You have hands, do it yourself." They started to threaten us that they would not give us any bread, but we did not care and said that we would not eat their bread. Then this colonel ordered to bring the fire hose. The spirit of God supported us, and we were ready even to be shot down. Finally, the colonel ordered us to go back to prison. "We did not come here and we will not go anywhere," we said. When they found out that none of us would obey their orders, they commanded to turn on the water and put the fire hose against our faces. After being tortured like that for two hours, half dead we were dragged back to prison where we thanked God for his mercy.

Shortly after that, a soldier came back and told us to prepare our meal, but we refused to eat and did not eat for eight days. At last, the doctors came and told us we were going to Fort Riley. As we could not move, many soldiers packed up our things and put us on wagons which carried us to the station. There they took us off and we were lying on the floor waiting for two hours for the next day. Now I am in the hospital and the others are in prison. They are forbidden to write in Russian. You write in English so that we will get your letters.

Good-bye, my dears. Pray God to give me strength to stand all the pains of my soul and body.

I will write more about what happened on the way. When we got here, they began to torture me like an animal with rope around my neck. That peeled the skin off my neck. They shaved my head, they cut my ears. They put a sabre to my neck. They tore my shirt in pieces and wanted me to put on a uniform. They threw me into an ice-cold bath. I did not count how many times they beat me. Once in one of those ice-cold baths I fainted and they took me out and tortured me again.

They pulled the hairs off my feet like feathers. I was motionless. I only prayed to God to take me away from this world full of horrors.

My hope and belief in God saved me.

Now I am preparing my meals, but I feel very ill.

Ivan Sussoff, Fort Riley, Kansas

The Molokans were transferred from Fort Riley to the U.S.D.B. at Fort Leavenworth. There they continued in their refusal to work and were placed in the dark solitary cells where they had to sleep on the cement floor with bedbugs and other vermin as their only companions. They were forbidden to write or talk, and were manacled to the cell door for nine hours a day.

Solitary prisoners were given bread and water for a two-week period, which was alternated with a regular diet for another two weeks. The Molokans, however, had it especially difficult because their religious scruples prevented them from eating the prison bread and many of the items on the regular diet. For many months they subsisted on corn flakes and milk, when allowed that. Eventually the army provided them with a special vegetable diet, but it was barely enough to subsist on.

Evan Thomas went to the prison commandant and told him that he could no longer work because it was the only way he could protest the treatment of the Molokans and the barbarities of the prison system. He was placed in solitary where he remained for two months.

Other prisoners who would not obey military orders, even in prison, or who wanted to join Evan in his sympathetic strike, were also placed in solitary.

These men received the same treatment and some of them were manacled to the doors of their cells with their backs to the door and their arms raised above their heads, an extremely painful position, for nine hours a day.

Sympathetic guards smuggled out letters, but the outside world treated their stories of torture with disbelief. Ironically, Howard Moore, while sub-humanly manacled to his cell door, received a Carnegie Medal for bravery for rescuing a drowning woman at the risk of his own life.

Clark Getts, a Chicago attorney, was placed in solitary for smuggling out information of the cruelties that were going on in the Fort Leavenworth U.S.D.B. When Captain Chambers, the prison psychiatrist, visited him after several weeks in solitary, Getts seemed too cheerful to him. So, the captain had him placed in a violent ward for observation, where he was in danger of his life and the patients mingled promiscuously.

According to a report of brutalities drawn up by Theodore H. Lunde, the father of Erling Lunde, and read on the floor of the House of Representatives by Charles H. Dillon, here are a few examples of other brutalities that took place:

10. Peters, No. 14589, Mennonite, from Fort Oglethorpe, Georgia. Lieut. Masey, when reading sentence, told him he was no longer a citizen, and therefore not entitled to hold his religious belief. Ordered to work at the point and prodding of the bayonet. Put in solitary under roof in barn, with only a small, square window for air, under a blazing August sun, on bread and water. Refusing to eat for five days, he fainted, was revived, and put back. Later taken to hospital totally demented and a wreck of a former splendid physique. Pneumonia, influenza, heart trouble, and a general breakdown. Finally discharged as mentally deficient....

Peters, mentioned above, saw the two following instances:

11. Detention camp, Fort Oglethorpe. Captain ordered soldiers to put C.O. waist deep in feces of latrine pit, splash him all over with the filth, sergeant in charge leaving him to be pulled out by his fellow C.O.s.

12. Same captain, same time, ordered C.O. Swartzendruber taken by the heels and dipped to his eyes in the feces of latrine pit. Sergeant proceeded to put him 'away in.' Peters warned him of danger of killing by suffocation before filth could be removed from mouth and nostrils.

13. Polish drafted deserter brought to Fort Oglethorpe during August. Had yellow jaundice. No food or medical attention for two days. Provost sergeant ordered him out to work under curses and oaths. Too sick to work. Sergeant ordered him to stand up; tried, but fell back on bunk. Sergeant grabbed and beat him; too exhausted. Sergeant called prison officer, Lieut. Masey, who grabbed and shook him viciously and ordered guard with fixed bayonet to force him out. Pole, leaning against wall for support, was jabbed four times in back with bayonet, until exhausted he fainted away. Taken to guardhouse and left on bunk for two days, until chaplain, Father Shear, came to call the mail. Duncan called the reverend father's attention to Pole's condition; he was horrified; said Lieut. Masey should be court-martialed, and threatened

to prefer charges. He only 'bawled him out,' preferring no charges. The Pole later died in the hospital as a direct result of cruel treatment....

19. Abraham Gelarter, vegetable dealer, orthodox Jew, Camp Upton to Fort Jay, April 11. Is greatly surprised and thanks his God for having survived the terrible punishments received for merely objecting to murder. The brutal sentries beat him until he was unable to recognize himself and encouraged the other prisoners to do the same. Commandant declared that all conscientious objectors deserved to be killed.

September 15, I arrived at Fort Leavenworth, and, being a vegetarian, had to go twice on hunger strike to get proper food, though far from adequate. Two periods of two weeks in solitary, handcuffed to cell nine hours per day. Compelled to bathe and shave on Saturday, my Sabbath. Dragged to the bath, knocked down, forcibly undressed, held under shower, and scrubbed with coarse soap. The brutalities of the soldiers made me scream with pain. I was taken out of the hole to the hospital November 22 for observation.

In the beginning of 1919, the War Department abandoned prolonged confinement in solitary cells for the purpose of breaking the wills of political prisoners. The death of the Hofer brothers at Fort Leavenworth probably had a lot to do with this.

Their story brings out the worst features of the authoritarian military and its prisons. The following account, which was printed by the American Industrial Company, Chicago (owned at the time by the father of Erling Lunde, one of the hunger strikers at Fort Riley) was carried to the outside world by an army officer. It is entitled "Crucifixion in the Twentieth Century, The Case of Jacob Wipf and the three Hofer Brothers, Religious Objectors to War, Two of whom died, from the effects of Military Atrocities in American Prisons, Told on the hospital cot by Jacob Wipf, who prays with Christ: 'Father, forgive them, for they know not what they do.' Fort Leavenworth, December 1918.

The fellow was telling his story. His eyes — plaintive eyes — spoke eloquently of intense suffering and were fitting comrades to the tale he voiced. The story, indeed, came as a stale breath from the Inquisition — a smudge of medievalism hanging on through the centuries to shadow its insidious deviltry upon our Twentieth Century — a hideous jest to taunt us moderns who boast of idealism and democracy.

Jacob Wipf and the three Hofer brothers were members of the
Hutterian sect. Staunch to their religious convictions, they protested
against the forced use of their bodies in war. They were remanded
by the authorities to the Alcatraz prison. This prison, built on a rock
island of twelve acres, contains a typical Spanish dungeon or "Hole" as
it is called in the vernacular of the prisoners. It is with this chamber of
punishment that our story deals.

...They believed, with an intense conviction, that their duty to
their God utterly precluded any submission to military command.
Immediately, therefore, upon their entrance to the prison they refused
to comply with any dictate of soldier authority.

Upon refusing to work, they were sentenced to confinement in the
Hole, and they descended to this terror cell to suffer for five days
under the most inconceivable conditions. The dungeon — a hideous
reminder of past ignorance and cruelty — is located thirty feet below
the base of the prison building and just at the level of the sea. The thick
stone walls, standing through long years, have become saturated with
moisture, and water continually worked through the crumbling mortar
joints and trickled on to the floor. The air of the place was heavy —
and always damp and stale.

Into this Hole the Hutterian Brothers were thrown and, impotent
before the uncompromising power the officers, they could not
reasonably anticipate help from any human agency. You cannot
conceive the poignant isolation an individual feels behind the walls
and restrictions of a military prison. A dull sodden impotence pervades
one's mind and body — a deep seated horror of the bars, the guards,
and the oppressive rules (regulations). Realizing the injustice of his
confinement and seeing his cherished American ideals of Freedom and
of the right to Honest Opinion brutally ravished — there comes to the
political prisoner a slow, throbbing spiritual pain. But add to this the
terrors of a torture cell of the Alcatraz type and you know the acme of
heinous persecution.

The four Hutterian were handcuffed by the wrists to an iron bar whose
level barely allowed their feet to touch the floor. Guards stripped them
of their civilian clothing down to underwear. Blankets or coverings of
any kind were refused them and they lived in shivering fear of the cold
and damp of the cell.

Besides them on the floor were laid soldier uniforms. The tenets of their church forbade the wearing of military garb. The sneering guards, miscalculating the determination of these prisoners, swore that soon they would be dressed up as "regular soldiers." Wipf's eyes shone triumphantly as he told me this incident.

"But," he said, "we decided to wear the uniform was not what God would have us do. It was a question of doing our religious duty and one of living or dying"; then quietly: "and we never wore the uniform."

For a full thirty-six hours, these quiet heroes remained "strung up" as it is called. Not a bite of food of any sort was furnished them and but one glass of water. They suffered — chilled to the bone, nearly naked, hungering and thirsting — add with pain and fatigue torturing their every nerve. To add to their torments, guards came to them during this 36-hour period and beat them brutally with clubs. Yet never once did they think of accepting the easy way out by succumbing to the military will.

Finally, the inhumanity — as well as the futility — of such treatment was apparent even to the authorities and they released the Hutterians who were, by this time, in wretched condition.

For the rest of the five-day period, they were exempt from this "hanging up" but the other features of the punishment remained in force. They were without clothing. The cell was damp and musty. They were allowed but a single glass of water each 24 hours and not a morsel of food for the full five days. The dungeon contained no bed and their rest was taken on the water-soaked floor. Washing and toilet facilities were entirely lacking and thus they were forced to live there close to the filth of their own excrement. Frequently the sentries came in to manhandle their victims.

Full of the horror and pain of it all, these four protestants to war gradually became physically weaker and weaker. They felt the "death by inches" close upon them. Sanity remained to them only by the sturdiest effort of will.

At last, the authorities, fearing the consequences of their action, released Wipf and the Hofers from this ordeal. They emerged from the dungeon, broken in health, and barely managing to walk. Upon reaching the light and fresh air of the upper prison, they were found to have contracted scurvy. Their skin was covered with unsightly eruptions. The effects of this disease were still evident in Wipf's face, as I talked with him.

This completes the story of the actual dungeon experience of the Hutterians, and, though they were yet exposed to many petty persecutions in the California prison, their lot was softened considerably.

The immediate sequel, however, is as hideous as the actual story. Shortly after their ordeal in the underground cell, the Hutterians were transferred to another military prison [ED. NOTE: Fort Leavenworth — U.S.D.B.] where most of the C.O.s are at present in confinement. The change was from a temperate climate to one more rigorous and this was accentuated because the season was that of early winter.

With their advent to the DISCIPLNE of this other prison, the Hutterians found similar difficulties awaiting them. They again refused to submit to military duties, and as in their former place of imprisonment, they were sentenced to confinement in solitary. Conditions here were infinitely more favorable in respect to sanitation and the like. Still, they were placed on a bread and water diet for fourteen days; strung up to the bars of their cell; and forced to sleep on the floor.

The consequences of such "disciplinary" treatment following so closely upon their former ordeal and combined with the sudden change from warm to cold weather are easily pictured. Cold draughts that swept across them as they slept on the floor soon took fatal effect on their weakened lungs. Within ten days two of them — two of the brothers — lay dead in the hospital. The immediate cause — the surgeon's report stated — was pneumonia!

The third brother — already in a precarious, though not, serious physical condition — was granted an immediate release, to arrange for the journey home of his dead brothers. Jacob Wipf — physically the strongest of the four — stayed staunchly in solitary fighting down his general weakness and diminishing vitality, with never a thought of playing the coward.

Finally, Wipf's physical strength became exhausted — and as I write his story, he now lies in the prison hospital suffering the effects of the dungeon torments. I recall him as he spoke with me, patient and quiet — though staunch in his unassuming heroism, he held neither malice nor hate against his oppressors. There was a gentle forgiveness for them. All that remained of his concern about his persecutions was a wonderment that our present system could thrive and that the social conscience could remain callous to such coercive brutalities.

This is the spirit of the man and the message of his story. It is sufficiently startling to quicken the conscience of every American to shame that he should be even remote party to such oppression. And similar sufferings were meted out to all the objectors to war, though in many instances the coercion was not carried to such brutal extremes as in the case of the Hutterians. But all suffered much the same — Christian and Jew — Socialist and Moralist — a thousand of them, and as clean cut and quietly brave group of Americans as I have ever seen teamed to a common cause.

You who are caught in the comfort of your library chair or the calm of your own firesides! You worshipers who sit softly in church and call the name of the Father! You workers and men of trade who are free to go and come as you will and to relax in the joy of your families! To all of you — Americans! — comes the story of Jacob Wipf and the Hofers who would not let their conscience die.

CHAPTER ELEVEN

Strike

We learned by way of the grapevine at Fort Riley guardhouse that the C.O.s who worked and soldier prisoners at the Fort Leavenworth Disciplinary Barracks (U.S.D.B.) had gone out on strike on January 29th.

Winthrop D. Lane, an editor of *The Survey*, by good fortune, had been at the U.S.D.B. at the time the strike was taking place. He had been commissioned by the National Civil Liberties Bureau to study prisons in which C.O.s and other political prisoners were confined. His report was published in *The Survey* for February 15, 1919.

Editors' note and strike summary: Max was transferred to the U.S.D.B shortly after the strike, but he included Lane's full article in his original text. It can be read in Appendix II. Included here is a summary of the strike by the editors and then two longer excerpts from Lane's article to tell the story:

On Wednesday afternoon, January 29, one work gang of 150 prisoners quit working, setting off a labor strike that eventually involved about 2,300 prisoners. The initial goals of the strike were unclear. As Lane wrote, "One prisoner wanted more tobacco; another wanted better food; another resented the treatment of Negroes on an equality with whites; a fourth felt bitter because he wasn't getting his letters from home; a fifth wanted the privilege of writing more letters himself."

Among the 150 was a conscientious objector, H. Austin Simons, who felt compelled to join the strike to maintain solidarity with all prisoners, but he wanted clear goals. After meetings with other C.O.s and prisoners, he played a role in helping to organize the strikers and outline demands. Strikers in each wing eventually formed committees and communicated among wings to share information.

That night a fire was set in the quartermaster's warehouse. Guards, nearby soldiers, and prisoners were all called to fight the fire, which caused about $100,000 in damage and increased tensions throughout the disciplinary barracks. Three prisoners later confessed to setting the fire. Although it was unclear if it was related to the strike, the fire further conveyed the general prisoner unrest and growing anger at prison conditions at the same time increasing apprehension among the guards and staff. Lane quotes the prison commandant Colonel Rice as saying, "This I.W.W. trouble that we have been fearing has started with some of the men."

On Thursday, January 30, the prisoners were sent back to their wings after breakfast rather than told to work, giving them time to continue organizing. Colonel Rice met with the prisoners in various sections and listened to their grievances of poor living conditions, rotting meat and poor food, and the inequality of their sentences. In the afternoon, as the strike continued, Rice met again with a large group of prisoners, asking to hear the prisoners' demands. With no chosen leader of the strike there was a general hesitancy by any one man to speak for the group until, as Lane writes in his article:

> Suddenly the ranks opened and a small prisoner [W. Oral James] with closely shaven head and wearing a long, ugly raincoat pushed forward. With his intent expression he had somewhat the appearance of a Franciscan monk. I had seen him at the Atlantic branch of the Disciplinary Barracks at Fort Jay and knew him to be the close friend and legal ward of a man long prominent in social work. An officer called: "Here is a speaker sir." There was a quick hush. Beginning in a low voice, the prisoner said:

"Sir, I have been here only a few days. I was transferred four days ago from the Disciplinary Barracks at Fort Jay. I am in no sense a leader of these men. I can speak for myself, however, and (here he raised his voice so that he could be heard throughout the yard), I think I can speak for many others in these silent ranks when I say that our object in thus seeming to oppose authority is that this the only way in which we can make articulate our demand to know what is to become of us. What, sir, is the government going to do with us?

"I am a conscientious objector. ... My own sentence happens to be twenty years, but my case is only one. There are hundreds of men in this prison bearing sentences of fifteen, twenty and twenty-five years (I am not now speaking of objectors only) who were new to military methods and requirements, and who committed offenses for which the peace-time judgments would be only a few months or at the most two or three years. Are those men to remain here for the rest of their lives?

"Sir, the armistice was signed nearly three months ago. The war is over, the government has already released 113 of our fellows. Has it not had time to investigate the justice of other claims?"

Friday, January 31, was the final day of the strike, and the rest of the strike story is excerpted here from Lane's article that Max had included in his manuscript:

The next morning no attempt was made to take the men out to work. Using my pass, I visited the men in the seventh wing. They received me as every body of men who think themselves unjustly treated receives a reporter — with open arms. To them I was bridge to the outside world. One prisoner suggested that I might be a government spy, but he was quickly silenced by those who thought they knew better. After all, they went largely on faith, for only one man in all these hundreds had known me personally before I had arrived a week earlier.

The men were just about to hold a meeting — the "soviet of the seventh wing," they were humorously calling themselves. Simons mounted a box and I leaned over the rail of the first balcony so that I could see the faces both above and below.

Simons was persuasive, eloquent, direct. His periods were rounded, his sentences complete, his climaxes effective. He told them that the strike had been organized in the other wings, each wing having elected a committee just as the seventh had done. He read the demands that had been formulated the night before: (1) that the commandant recommend to the War Department the immediate release of all military prisoners; (2) immunity from punishment for all men who had led in the strike movement; (3) recognition of a permanent grievance committee of prisoners.

He told them that theirs was the just cause of self-government now being fought for throughout the civilized world. He brought prolonged applause by his dramatic announcement that the disciplinary battalion (the group of men about to be restored to the service) had joined the strike, and though this news later proved to be untrue, the reception accorded it showed how eagerly the men welcomed additions to their ranks. He declared that no authority could withstand the power of a united body of men. Efforts, he said, would be made to separate them.

"When the officials come to take you out of your wings," he shouted, "use no violence. Whether they take you out together, in groups, or singly, go quietly into the yard. Once there, refuse to work. Violence accomplishes nothing. Solidarity accomplishes all things. The watchword of the working-men throughout the world today is solidarity. Say nothing, do nothing, but stand like this." The speaker folded his arms. "A man who commits no overt act, but stands like this, is immovable."

As he spoke, I thought of the thousand soldiers outside. I thought of the thick walls that shut these men in, and of the barred doors between them and their fellows. I wondered what was the mysterious power by which the speaker and his listeners thought they could control their own destinies. There seemed a grim and tragic humor in the situation of these upturned faces, eagerly drinking in the word of their interpreter. I wondered if either he or they fully sensed the dire possibilities that seemed so imminent to me.

I returned to the prison offices with this question in my mind. There I learned that Colonel Rice, after a sleepless night, had made up his mind. He called me into his office and asked me to sit down. I could see at once that his struggle had been intense. He went quickly to the heart of his decision. He had enough force at his command, he said, to compel obedience from every prisoner. "No one knows better than I," he declared, "what this might mean. It might mean violence and it might mean bloodshed. If these men were merely mutinous, I should not hesitate. But this is no ordinary prison uprising. These men have some justification, much justification, for their feeling of discontent. I know the approved military method of handling this situation, but I know, too, that we are in a changed world today. The American people do not stand for the use of military force if there is a better way. I propose to find that better way. I shall listen to a committee of prisoners. If this is surrender, let them make the most of it."

I felt that he had reached a momentous decision. A moment later I realized just how courageous his decision was. An officer of Colonel Rice's staff stopped me and said:

"Do you know how to settle this mutiny?"

"No" I answered.

"'Well, I do,' he snapped. "I could settle it in seventy-two hours. I'd lock every prisoner in his cell and I'd starve him, that's what I'd do. In three days every one of 'em would be crawling to me on their bellies, begging to be allowed to work. A week'd see them. I'm plumb disgusted with this pusillanimous way of handling a bunch of criminals."

The committee met with the commandant and several other officers at 2:30 that afternoon. When the seventeen prisoners marched into the room, Colonel Rice asked them if they had a spokesman. Simons stepped forward. He said:

"Sir, on behalf of the general prisoners confined in this barracks, I am authorized to present to you the following statement of demands, which I shall read:

"We the men now confined in the U.S.D.B., Fort Leavenworth, Kansas, having been convicted by court-martial, present the following as essential for the restoration of normal conditions:

1. That the commandant immediately release from solitary confinement all men now there for having participated in this movement from its beginning, and that he promise that no man involved in this movement shall be punished or discriminated against in the future for his part in it.

2. That the following telegram be sent to the Secretary of War at once: "General prisoners confined in the U.S.D.B., Fort Leavenworth, petition, with approval of commandant, for amnesty to all convicted by court-martial. Senators Chamberlain and Borah, American Bar

97

Association and public opinion generally declare sentences unjust and amnesty the proper redress. Our release is just as urgent as that of the 113 conscientious objectors recently discharged. Democratic military justice requires amnesty. (Signed) Prisoners' General Committee elected at request of officers.

3. That the commandant recognizes a permanent grievance committee to be elected by the men; and that this committee shall have the right to discuss with the authorities such improvements of conditions as seem in the committee's judgment to be desirable.

Colonel Rice took up the points one by one. The first, in spite of its somewhat vague phraseology, was well known to refer particularly to white prisoners who had been placed in solitary confinement for participating in the race riots. Colonel Rice told the committee that eleven of the men so confined had already been released and that the cases of the other three were at that moment being investigated by the executive officer. A new man held this position, "Square Deal" Smith, so called from his record of fairness in the navy. After some parleying, the committee decided to present those facts to the men and to seek their judgment.

It was now Colonel Rice's turn to explode a bombshell. At last, he took the men into his confidence. He read a paragraph from a letter that he had sent to the War Department a month previously on the question of excessive war-time sentences urging that they be reduced to a peace-time basis. This would cut many 15-, 20- and 25-year sentences to a few months, or at most to a year or two. It was evident that the members of the committee were greatly surprised at this revelation of the commandant's action. They stood, however, for the sending of the telegram. Colonel Rice offered instead to deliver the message in person, and explained that he was making an official trip to Washington in two days. To this the committee finally agreed. It agreed also to omit the words, "With approval of commandant," since by taking the message in person Colonel Rice gave evidence of his approval.

The third point caused no difficulty whatever, for Colonel Rice immediately said that he would be entirely willing to discuss matters with a general prisoners' committee, so long as such a committee displayed a proper sense of leadership and remained representative of the men.

The men returned to their wings. They were given an hour — all they asked for — in which to report the decision of the other prisoners.

Rumors quickly came back that the committee was meeting with difficulty in some of the wings. The fourth wing, especially, we heard, was insisting that the message to the Secretary of War be sent at once by wire. The reason was not far to seek. The strike could then be continued until an answer had been received!

At last, the committee returned, four hours after its appointment. A new spokesman stepped to the front.

"Sir, I am spokesman this evening, general prisoner 17380, who acted as spokesman this afternoon being somewhat tired."

Thus spoke Carl Haessler, graduate of the University of Wisconsin, Rhodes Scholar at Oxford, editorial writer, socialist, conscientious objector. He continued:

"Sir, I have to report that the general prisoners confined in this barracks have voted unanimously — unanimously, sir — to return to work tomorrow morning and to restore a normal state of affairs upon the conditions agreed upon this afternoon."

A breath could have been heard. Colonel Rice's eyes softened, his face became suffused with emotion, and he said almost in a whisper, "That is very, very gratifying."

The strike was over. The democratic, non-military method had won. And the members of the 49th Infantry, who had been cooling their heels outside the gates for two days, were sent packing.

Chapter Twelve

Disciplinary Barracks

New York Times, March 30, 1919

HOW LEAVENWORTH GOT ITS OBJECTORS

Path of the Conscientious Avoiders of Military Duty to the Penitentiary.

TOLD IN OFFICIAL PAPERS

Modifications of Military Practice Ordered by Newton Baker on President's Ruling.

OVER ANSELL'S OBJECTION

Result, with Observations on Conduct of His Charges, Reported by Sergt. Alexander.

"… the defiant attitude of the objectors and of their efforts to convert their guards to socialism.… Some of the ringleaders, troublemakers, and agitators at the camp who led this strike and who had been moving spirits in friction and grief at the tent colony were: Conscientious Objectors Henry Monski, Evan W. Thomas, Samuel Solnitsky, Julius Katz, Jacob Worsman, Herman Block, David Eichel, Erling Lunde, Emanuel Silver, Ulysses de Rosa, John Downey, Joseph Brandon, Francis Steiner, Frank J. Burke, Morris Franklin, Max Sandin, Jacob Haugan, and Lester G. Ott. …"

HOW LEAVENWORTH GOT ITS OBJECTORS

Path of the Conscientious Avoiders of Military Duty to the Penitentiary.

———

TOLD IN OFFICIAL PAPERS

———

Modifications of Military Practice Ordered by Baker on President's Ruling.

———

OVER ANSELL'S OBJECTION

———

Result, with Observations on Conduct of His Charges, Reported by Sergt. Alexander.

———

Sergeant Merrill Alexander, one of the non-commissioned officers who were in charge of the conscientious objectors first at Fort Leavenworth, and later at Fort Riley, wrote in the form of an official communication just before he was discharged from the army his own personal observations and experiences with these men, most of whom were subsequently released from duty with honorable discharges, and look now for the

O n February 17, 1919, I was transferred to the U.S.D.B., a few days after the strike was over. This was my second trip to this prison. When we approached the prison doors this time it did not seem to me that they are so large as they looked my first time back in June when I had only been two weeks in the camps. Now, I had the experience of seven months in the camps and guardhouses. I knew all about the strike in this prison. I knew that many C.O.s were refusing to work and they were living in Cantonment No. 7 outside the prison stonewalls, where there were no more "literary" cells, no more announcements of "No supper tonight," and no more "cold baths."

The prison officer who interviewed me said that from now on I would not be known as "Private Sandin" but as number "16299." He asked me what kind of work I could do. I told him that I would not work while in prison. "But all the C.O.s are working here," he assured me. I knew this to be a lie from the grapevine at Fort Riley.

"Put prisoner 16299 in the hole on bread and water," and they marched me down to the fourth wing sub-basement and locked me in a solitary cell. Even though manacling had been abandoned by the War Department, I was chained to the door with my hands up, and the guards pulled off my shoes and socks and locked the door. The room was about 5 feet high. I am 5 feet 2 inches tall so I could not keep my head up when I was handcuffed to the door. I could not move, lie down or walk around. I was in this position until the next morning without food or water. In the morning the guards opened the door and unlocked my hands and I fell on the floor.

> *"I was chained to the door with my hands up. The room was about 5 feet high so I could not keep my head up. I could not move, lie down or walk around. I was in this position until the next morning without food or water."*

On the first page of a booklet which was given to me entitled "Special Regulations for the Government and Discipline of General Prisoners," I learned that my total sentence was now fifteen years and no months. "Your allowance of good time is 4 years 10 months. You can lose all or part of it by misconduct. It is not yours unless you earn it by constant good behavior. If you lose no good time your sentence expires 3/24/1929. You were convicted of disobedience of orders.... You will be eligible to apply for release in home parole 7/24/1926."

This was the first official notice that I had received of my sentence. While I knew officially for several months that I had been sentenced to be shot, I gathered now from this booklet that my sentence had been commuted to fifteen years.

The booklet, titled "Schooling and Vocational Training," stated:

It is the policy of those in charge of this institution to do everything that may help to send you away from here a better man than when you came.

They are striving to so conduct this institution that every man who leaves it will be:

Improved in morals.

Improved in mind and education.

Improved in body.

And able to earn more money than when he entered the gates to begin serving his sentence.

Note carefully and read again the above words.

To be able to earn more money.

Do you want to do that?

You are now in detention here, one of about three thousand whose lives have been more or less failures up to this time. Your failure and theirs were due to a considerable extent to bad morals, to a lack of education, or to a lack of vocational training.

Do you wish to improve here or not? Have you any desire left in you to become a success after leaving here? Or don't you care? Ask yourself these questions when you are alone and carefully think out the answer. Face the truth.... If you work faithfully and do your best when given the opportunity, you will go out a better man than when you came in, able to earn more money. Is that worthwhile? To anyone who values himself, it is. Is it to you?...

If you are given the job you request and do not work faithfully, nor behave yourself, you will be removed at once and a better man put in your place. There are always enough good willing workers to fill the best places, so when you get one, "get on your toes" and show that there is something in you. Earn the good opinion of your foreman. It may be worth dollars to you in the future.

The commandant's desire is that every man confined here do his duty from a sense of honor and that every man prove himself worthy of trust.

Some people may say that men in this institution are without honor. Show them that they are wrong!

Do you care? Which do you choose, to be spoken of by your foreman and officers as a "good man" or as "no good?" Does it make any difference to you? It should for your own sake if for no other reason.

WHAT DOES HONOR MEAN?
This is what it means:
A chance here.
Shorter time to serve.
More money outside.

WHAT DOES DISHONOR MEAN?
Less chance here.
Longer time to serve.
Less money outside.

The next morning, I was interviewed again by Colonel Rice, who said, "Now, 16299, you are in a real prison. You will have to spend many years of your life here. So, better try your best and be a good prisoner. I have your record since you have been in the Army and it is not so good. We have law and order here and punishments for those who break discipline. Now tell me, what kind of work would you like to do?"

Once more I told him that I could not work while in prison.

"Take No. 16299 and put him in cantonment No. 7 with the rest of those crazy nuts," he ordered a guard.

Cantonment No. 7 was a stockade behind the U.S.D.B. where most of the C.O.s had been placed after the strike in order to isolate them from the rest of the prison population. The other prisoners were told that we were placed there because we were crazy.

The C.O.s named the stockade "Wire City." There were no guards inside of the cantonment and we were free to do what we wanted. We organized classes in English, foreign languages, American history, etc. I sometimes substituted for Howard Moore as grammar instructor. We had plenty of time for games and for arguing about the direction of the Russian revolution.

I remember one day when several high officers were inspecting the cantonment, one of them saw our bulletin board with a schedule of classes on it. He said in disgust, "Hell, they are not in prison. They are in college."

Even though we had freedom to do what we wanted within the cantonment, there was still that wire fence and the armed guards on the outside, which prevented us from going home to our loved ones.

During these past months 504 conscientious objectors had been tried by courts-martial. Of these only one was acquitted (although three were later disapproved by reviewing authority and 50 on recommendation of the Judge Advocate General).

According to a table given by Assistant Secretary of War Keppel in "Statement Concerning Conscientious Objectors," p. 51, Exhibit 31, the following "Original Sentences of Courts" had been handed out to C.O.s:

Death	17	Less than one year	3
Life	142	2 years	3
10 years	89	50 years	3
20 years	73	8 years	1
25 years	57	11 years	1
15 years	47	12 years	1
5 years	29	13 years	1
30 years	19	18 years	1
3 years	5	28 years	1
1 year	4	45 years	1
40 years	4	99 years	1
		Total	503

None of the death or longer sentences were ever carried out. The government was slowly and haphazardly going about the job of reducing these sentences. But as far as we knew we had many long years ahead of us in the military prisons. On March 4, 1919, the following article appeared in the *New York Times*:

> Disapproval by President Wilson of the death sentence imposed by a military court-martial upon Private Max Sandin, a conscientious objector at Camp Funston, Kansas, was announced today by the War Department. A sentence of fifteen years was approved.
>
> Sandin was found guilty of having refused to obey an order of his superior officer to clean up a pile of refuse in the camp.
>
> Major General Leonard Wood, commanding at Camp Funston at the time of the trial, recommended that the sentence be commuted to confinement at hard labor, in view of the fact that at the present time the ends of discipline of this command do not demand the execution of the extreme penalty.

I was relieved to see this news item because the government had kept me in the dark all these months as to my official status. I had learned from a guard that I was to be shot and from a prison handbook that my sentence had apparently been reduced to 15 years, but now, although from a newspaper, I knew definitely what my status was.

Life in the cantonment went on as usual. Every evening we had a story hour. Each C.O. would have his turn some evening to tell the story of his life. We put out a newspaper called the *Wire City Weekly*, which was typed by the C.O.s who went to work in the prison office. The paper was a satire on prison life, on ourselves, and the officers. Unfortunately, the prison officials found out about it after only six or seven issues.

Another time the officers thought they were punishing us by putting Negroes in with us. But they were a big help as they had been in the other guardhouses, because they went out to work and were able to smuggle out our letters and in cigarettes, writing paper, candy, etc.

About a week before May Day, we decided to have a May Day celebration in Wire City, with speeches and a parade. Our plans were found out, and many of us were transferred to the guardhouse at Fort Leavenworth.

That evening a captain thought that his order for quiet had not been obeyed quickly enough, so he had us drenched with pounding water from a fire hose. The water continued all night long. We climbed into the upper bunks for protection. When the barrage finally stopped, everything in the guardhouse was drenched and the floor had several feet of water on it.

We remained in the guardhouse for about two days with water-soaked mattresses and damp clothing.

When we returned to Wire City, we were glad to learn that the May Day celebration had taken place anyway with many of the religious C.O.s joining in.

One day, I received a notice that my sentence had been reduced to 18 months. It would now be the summer of 1920 before I would be able to breath fresh air again.

On June 22, I received a notice informing me that I did not have to work that day (of course, I would not have worked anyway). I jumped with joy because I knew that such notices were issued the day before a prisoner was to be released. I could hardly believe it. I began to remove the number 16299 from a pair of pants and a shirt.

After a sleepless night, I was called to the prison offices where a clerk gave me $390 in back pay and told me to sign army discharge papers. When I told him I did not want the money and I could not sign the papers, he rolled his eyes as if to say that I really was from an insane asylum.

"I cannot sign a discharge from an army that I have never considered myself a part of, and I cannot accept money because I am a worker, and I only accept money when I do useful work for the community. This is a soldier's pay, and a soldier does no useful work for the community. He is paid to kill and to destroy the community of man."

"I do not know what to do with you," the clerk said. "I guess you will have to go back to prison."

The next day, June 24th, I was summoned to the prison offices again. The clerk gave me the discharge papers unsigned, a civilian jacket and pants, and $5.

At the bottom of the discharge, the following was written: "This man is a conscientious objector who has done no military duty whatsoever and who refuses to wear the uniform. Signature of soldier _____. Is not recommended for reenlistment."

After saying goodbye to my comrades — I was sorry to leave them behind — a guard led me and three other C.O.s to the big iron gates of the U.S.D.B. They were opened for us, and we walked out into the free Kansas land, four victorious men.

Sandin death sentence commuted, The Fairfield Journal, *Fairfield, IA, March 7, 1919*

Part Three:
Interbellum

CHAPTER THIRTEEN

Back in Cleveland

When I arrived home in Cleveland, I was happily surprised to find about thirty members of the Young People's Socialist League waiting at the railroad station to greet me. They took me to the Labor Lyceum where two hundred more of my friends were waiting. They called me their peace hero, the *people's soldier* who practiced what he preached.

For the next several months, whenever I walked, down the street, people would point me out "There he goes," they would say, "the socialist who refused to wear a soldier's uniform."

One day, when I went into Cohen's restaurant on Woodland Avenue for lunch, a crowd gathered about my table. Mr. Cohen came over to me and said "Mr. Sandin, please, come in here every day for the next month and I will feed you three meals a day without charge. When you come into my restaurant, it fills up."

"Thank you," I said, "I will accept your offer if you will let me do K.P."

"What is this?" he asked indignantly, thinking that I would want to wash dishes in return for his favor.

I don't know if I reassured him when I replied, "Kiss Peggy, your niece."

My reception in Cleveland was not entirely favorable. When I asked the real estate man for whom I had papered houses before the war and who had been one of my witnesses for my citizenship papers for work, he said: "Max, I know you are an honest man who suffered for a principle, but I don't agree with you. I am an American, and you can't work for me anymore." He said that he had received a letter from Mr. Newton Baker, the Secretary of War (and former mayor of Cleveland), requesting information about me, and that he had told him exactly what he had told me.

The government had also written to my other witness, Mr. Rabb, a builder, wanting to know how he could recommend a man such as me for citizenship. He stood up for me, however, and replied that I was an honest worker and a good socialist.

On July 17, 1919, the Young People's Socialist League, with the cooperation of Branch 1 of the Socialist Party and Branch 79 of the Workmen's Circle, held a banquet in my honor. There were about five hundred guests at Emery Hall that evening and plenty of toasts, speeches, praise, good wishes, and hot kisses from the Mrs. and Misses. Charles Ruthenberg was the main speaker.

All the speakers agreed that I had taken the right stand in refusing to cooperate — all but Bernard Tamerkin, who later was a spokesman for the Proletarian Party. He felt that class-conscious workers should infiltrate the ranks of the army to propagandize the evil and uselessness of war. Such action, he felt, would be stronger than the action, however courageous, of one individual not cooperating. (I met Mr. Tamerkin by chance many years later in Florida. I told him of my book, and he suggested the title, "I Was Sentenced to Be Shot.")

Shortly after I returned home to Cleveland, I wrote the following letter to Newton Baker:

> On Tuesday, June 24, 1919, I was released from the United States
> Disciplinary Barracks at Fort Leavenworth. Will you let me know,
> please, why I am free when many of my comrades are still in prison?
> I was an absolutist and refused all noncombatant service — I never
> worked in the disciplinary barracks because I could not recognize

military authority. But many who were still there were willing to accept farm furloughs and they also worked in prison; why then was I the one to go? I feel they are entitled to freedom as much as I. Why can they not be freed at once?

This letter was printed in the radical religious journal, *The World Tomorrow*, with the following editorial comment:

We are glad to print Mr. Sandin's letter, which gives new proof of the refusal of the War Department to deal honestly and liberally with the problem of conscientious objectors. Lately they have transferred one of objectors to the prison on Alcatraz Island and another group to the internment camp at Ft. Douglas, Utah. These men were handcuffed like dangerous criminals throughout the long trip and according to reliable information three of them have suffered solitary confinement in the black filthy dungeon at Alcatraz where the Hofer Brothers endured such agonies. At Ft. Douglas conditions are in every way better then Ft. Leavenworth, but the time has come not for an alleviation of prison conditions, but for a general amnesty for all political prisoners.

The government's actions were puzzling. One C.O. was sentenced to be shot after the armistice had been signed. C.O.s who had been charged and tried for similar infractions received different reductions in their sentences. At Fort Douglas, the commandant insisted in using military commands in getting the C.O.s to work. Most of them refused and were placed in solitary confinement. Howard Moore was brutally beaten in solitary when he refused to clean out his cell when ordered to do so. The government took away good time from those who refused to work.

At Fort Leavenworth U.S.D.B., the prisoners went out on strike again on July 21, 1919. The immediate cause of the strike was the wretched food, but underlying this, the prisoners, many of whom had just returned from France, were smarting at severe court-martial sentences and brutal treatment in the guardhouses. (Some of them had received long sentences for merely talking with German women.)

Their demands for a general amnesty, better food, and more tobacco, were wired to Washington, and they were told that they wouldn't have to work until an answer was received. The next morning, however, those who wanted to work were not permitted to do so by the prison authorities. Squads of men and machine guns were placed in the yard, armed sentries inside the wings, and the men were placed on bread and water. They were told that no man would be permitted to work until all agreed to do so.

One "officer and gentleman" took pot shots at the prisoners with his automatic. Soldiers in the yard periodically fired their rifles at the windows of the wings. The strike was broken after a week. Having won, the authorities retaliated by continuing these men on a restricted diet of bread and water for a while, cancelling all privileges — including a day of rest and recreation in the yard — increasing the work hours, and, worst of all, taking away all good time from the prisoners — including those who had wanted to work during the strike.

The government, apparently, had welcomed this strike, which it called a "mutiny" as an excuse to return to the old iron rule. Unfortunately, none of the leaders of the original strike were left in the prison. Needless to say, the prisoners' committee was abolished.

One of the most dramatic incidents began in July 1920, when the C.O. who had been preparing food for Ben Salmon, a Catholic C.O., had been released from Fort Douglas. Salmon, who objected to preparing his own food while being held by the military, went on a hunger strike. He was transferred to a mental hospital in Washington, D.C. The doctors there took three months before they decided to judge Salmon sane. Under the pressure of a habeas corpus proceeding introduced by the National Civil Liberties Bureau on Salmon's behalf, the War Department released Salmon in November. He had not eaten anything voluntarily during that time.

On November 23, 1920, two years after the end of the war, the last of the C.O.s were released by the military. Not so lucky, were several of the political prisoners who had been convicted under the espionage law. They had to remain in civilian prisons for several more years.

Back in Cleveland, my attention turned to love. I asked Sarah Madow, who I had known in YPSL before the war, if she would take a trip with me to Detroit. She accepted on the condition that I be a gentleman, which I promised. On the way to Detroit, we stopped in a small town to ask a man for directions. He told us, and then he asked me what my number was. I said 16299. Luckily, Sarah corrected me, and the man, who was a detective suspicious of us as strangers with a new Model T Ford, did not recognize it as a prison number.

I married Sarah Madow on August 28, 1920. We moved into our own house on 119th Street, which I had built in 1916.

The day after of our wedding, we were overjoyed to receive the following telegram from some of my prison colleagues who were still being detained!

August 29, 1920
FORT DOUGLAS, UTAH
MAX SANDIN
3465 EAST ONE HUNDRED AND NINETEENTH ST.
CLEVELAND O CAPITAL M. OUR HEARTFELT SINCERE
WISHES GO OUT TO YOU BERNSTEIN GREENBERG
LASSEN MOORE PLATIN BREIDERT POWELL FRANKLIN
STEINER SILVER STERENSTEIN CLAVE KATZ HAUGEN.

Now that I had a wife and house and car to upkeep, I decided, against my conscience, to go into business. I resigned from the Painters' Union and became a contractor hiring three men at the union wage of $40 per week.

After three months, I made an accounting of my books and found that I had made a net profit of $70 per week. I could not sleep. My conscience bothered me. Finally, I gave up my exploitation of these men and once again was a failure.

On July 14, 1921, our first child was born. We did not go to dead ancestors for a name for her. We chose "Irene," which means peace.

When Irene was in the fifth grade, she was transferred into a program for exceptional children at the Paul Revere School. She attended Western Reserve College for one year and Ohio University in Athens for another. In 1947, she married Perry Tenenbaum, who was studying law. He is now a lawyer, and they have a little girl, Debbie. We live in the same house.

Our second child was born on August 7, 1924. We named him Carl after Karl Liebknecht.

When our boy was about three years old, he showed signs of something being wrong with him. We called many doctors and took him to several hospitals, and they all said that nothing was wrong with him physically. When he reached school age, the school doctor told us that Carl was mentally retarded and that they could not take him in the school.

In 1929, we took him to Johns Hopkins Hospital in Baltimore. The doctors told us that there were many like him and that there was no remedy or hope for them. No operation would help these unfortunates.

We sent Carl to a private school for about five years. The school was about six miles from our home and three transfers on the street car line. His mother would take him to school, come back home to do the housework, and then go back to school to bring him home again. She spent about four hours a day on street cars.

The money that we spent on his schooling would have paid his way through medical school. It was throwing money away. Nothing was accomplished.

When Carl grew up, he became a problem. What could we do with him? He was a nice, quiet boy, but he was too big to play with five- or six-year-olds who were on his mental level. The older boys used to make fun of him. We could not keep him at home all the time, and it would not be safe to leave him alone in the street. Finally, we decided that the best thing we could do was to send him to a state school,

We made an application through the probate court. After waiting several months, we received notice that he had been accepted for the state school, brought him to the probate court to sign the papers, but the judge told us that there was a long waiting list of about four hundred children.

On the way out of the courtroom, someone pulled me aside and said that it would take five years or more before my boy would be at the top of the waiting list. He then told me that a thousand dollars would make it possible for Carl's name to be moved to the top,

I told him that I did not have a thousand dollars and that if I did, I would not pay a bribe to anybody.

"If you change your mind, I will be here," he replied. "Politics or money goes a long way."

What could we do? We had a sick child, thirteen years old. There were hundreds more like him. And somebody was making a business of that misery.

A family lived across the street from us with a ten-year-old boy who could not get out of his bed. He had been lying in filth and the house stank so that no one could stay in it very long. I wondered how long he and others like him would have to wait to be taken care of in a state institution while those with a thousand dollars were placed ahead of them.

I mentioned our plight at a labor meeting, Afterwards, a high official of the American Federation of Labor told me to come to his office the next morning. When I arrived, his secretary handed me a closed envelope and told me to take it down to the judge's secretary at the probate court.

1 do not know what was in that envelope, but I gathered that politics were involved because two weeks later I received a letter from the court telling me to take my boy to the state school at Columbus.

I never said thanks to anybody, because I did not know then and do not know now who was responsible for my boy's admission. But my conscience bothers me. I know that you don't get something for nothing when it comes to politics; and I understand that the official who had given me the letter had endorsed that judge when he was running for office. I felt that my boy's admittance to the school a form of a bribe to the politicians.

But it was the only way I could help my boy. I could not keep him. If my wife and I died he would have to be taken away anyway. If there would be a question of my life, I would be ready to give it for my child, but it could not be done, so I was forced to accept a favor.

In 1956, he was transferred from Columbus to Apple Creek in Wooster, Ohio. At that time the state sent me a bill for $4,000 for his upkeep, which I could not pay. I have received many letters from the state attorney general in spite of the fact that I have told him I could not pay such a large sum.

We visit our boy every month and take him home one month every year. He is a very nice, quiet boy, and when I take him back, he starts to cry saying, "Daddy, it isn't my fault," and he is shivering all the time on the road back. If, by some miracle, I could change places with him, I would gladly accept it.*

---

*Carl Sandin died at age 81 in Wellington, Ohio, where he had lived for some decades. An obituary was printed in the Cleveland Plain Dealer on June 25, 2006, stating he had worked at the Murray Ridge Production Center and retired in the late 1990s, and that "He enjoyed people watching, music and shared his peaceful soul with everyone who touched his life."

Chapter Fourteen

A Dissenting Voice

While I was in prison, most debates and arguments centered around the recent victorious October 1917 Russian revolution. At Fort Riley we named our tent "Smolny Institute," while other tents were named "Red Worker," "Workers' Freedom," "Tent Lenin," and "Tent Trotsky." We were divided into different groups each with their own Hero of the Russian Revolution. At that time, I could not decide who was who, so I stayed away from any particular group.

When I returned to Cleveland, the Socialist movement was divided into "right" and "left" wings, and each wing was preaching the thinking that they were the real revolutionist. The arguments went so far that words were not always enough, so fists and chairs were frequently used. The most common word was "anti-revolutionist."

The left wingers wanted to transform the Socialist Party into a revolutionary Leninist organization. The right-wing leaders of the Socialist Party proceeded to expel or suspend many left-wing-led branches. Eventually, many left wingers gave up the party and formed several rival communist groups.

I was too busy getting married, starting a family, and working in my paper-hangers' local to become involved in these factional struggles, which were over my head anyway and didn't interest me in the least. Although I was disappointed that the anti-war resolution of 1917 had been watered down or abandoned by many Socialist Party leaders as the war went on, I remained in the party for a while. (Victor Berger, Morris Hillquit, who had introduced the resolution at the convention, Meyer London, and others had become war supporters; Eugene Debs was one of the few who had remained true to the resolution, and consequently received a ten-year prison sentence for violating the Espionage Act.) I was nominated a delegate to the state convention in 1920, at which I was chosen one of 24 electors from the State of Ohio for Eugene Debs for President of the United States.

Ever since the advent of the "Great" War, and especially after the enactment of the Espionage Act of June 15, 1917, the policy of the Wilson administration toward dissident groups was one of repression. And the rest of the country took up the battle.

The Industrial Workers of the World (IWW) was especially hard hit. Seventeen IWWs were tarred and feathered in Tulsa, Oklahoma. Frank Little, a crippled IWW leader, was hanged from a railroad trestle in Butte, Montana. Over a thousand IWW strikers in Bisbee, Arizona, were herded into a ball park, packed into cattle cars, and dumped in the desert. The government simultaneously raided every major Industrial Worker hall in the country and arrested 166 leaders on a charge of violating the Espionage Act.

The Socialist Party magazine, *The American Socialist*, was banned from the mails, as was almost every radical publication, by the end of 1917. In addition to Eugene Debs, Victor Berger, the party's national secretary, was convicted under the Espionage Act, as were Charles Ruthenberg, Bill Haywood, Max Eastman, John Reed, and many others.

Several professors were dismissed by Columbia University because they had criticized the government's policy. Charles Beard resigned in protest. After the war, Harold Studley Gray tried to enter Columbia to finish his studies but was denied entrance because he was a conscientious objector. The dean told him that people of his view colored the university and made it difficult to raise funds. Gray was admitted to Harvard.

A twenty-year-old girl, Nellie Steimer, received a fifteen-year sentence in 1918 for passing out leaflets against Allied intervention in Russia.

After the war, the country turned its attention to the "red menace."

Streamers proclaiming "Kill Bolshevism or Be Killed" were placed on Cleveland's streetcars during the Victory Loan campaign of 1919. Attorney General A. Mitchell Palmer was conducting his famous "red" raids.

While I was being drenched by water in the guardhouse at Fort Leavenworth on May Day 1919, five thousand Clevelanders stayed home from work to conduct a May Day parade. Charles Ruthenberg, then Socialist Party candidate for mayor, led the parade of men, women, and children who wore red badges and carried red banners or American flags.

There were thirty men in army uniforms in the parade. At one point an onlooker yelled to the uniformed marchers, "Take off that uniform." A number of spectators rushed toward the marchers and a fight was on.

Two policemen arrived on the scene. "Both wielded their maces vigorously and several persons were injured," one news story reported. The mounted police came, and while the horses and men succeeded in driving many of the marchers onto the sidewalks, about five hundred of them reached the Public Square.

Several of the Socialist speakers mounted a platform that had been erected for the Victory Loan campaign. An Army lieutenant jumped onto the platform and seized a red banner. According the newspapers he was attacked and scores of men jumped onto the platform to come to his aid.

Fights broke out all over. The army lieutenant and a police detective were fighting each other, thinking that the other was a Socialist.

One of the red flags was burned in the square. Anybody wearing a red badge was attacked. The marchers who had been stopped by the mounted police were also attacked. A police sergeant was shot in the thigh while attempting to stop a fight.

Every picture and piece of furniture in the Socialist Party headquarters on Prospect Avenue was broken. A mob led by two sailors attacked Acme Hall where the Socialists had assembled for the parade. One man who was seated in a cafe attached to the hall with his wife and daughter was dragged into the street and severely beaten.

Socialists who had gathered in front of Acme Hall were told to move on by a detective. One of the men hit him, according to reports, and the detective shot the man with his pistol, killing him.

Another Socialist Party hall on Lorain Avenue was ransacked by another mob. Police swung their maces through a crowd of six hundred, which was gathering near the hall. Five people were hurt.

Charles Ruthenberg was arrested. The Socialists claimed that the rioting was started by members of the Loyal American League, spectators, and soldiers. The police claimed that the marchers started it by attacking the patrolman.

The newspapers condoned the mob's conduct and one said in an editorial that the people in the mob were American and patriots to the core. And the police said in condemning the Socialists that "The people gave us wonderful support."

At one point the Labor Lyceum, which we YPSLs had cared for before the war, had been broken into and wrecked. Every single book was thrown on the floor and all furniture and windows smashed.

I left the Socialist Party with fifty others from my Jewish branch No. 1 late in 1921 to join the newly formed Workers Party (the early name of the Communist Party). I felt that the Communists would bring socialism to this country faster than the right-wing Socialist Party. Many of the more militant socialists, who had remained true to the anti-war resolution of 1917, were now in the Workers Party. Charles Ruthenberg was its first executive secretary.

It took me several years to find out that there was a gap between the ideals of Communism and the practices of Communists (as there is between the ideals and practices of right wingers also). I found many Communists to be selfish persons trying to get some gain for themselves in the form of jobs. I could not tolerate this selfishness and pointed out their faults, mistakes and crimes. Of course, they did not like this. One woman once told me that they would have a benefit for me to send me to California if I would stay there.

I do not intend to go into the details of my disillusionment, because Communists are subject to vicious attacks in this country, and I have no intention of providing the government or anyone else with fodder for such attacks. I will only mention several personal experiences I had while connected with the party that will touch upon the reasons for my disillusionment.

When the split came between the Socialists and the Communists, the executive committee of the Workmen's Circle (a Jewish fraternal order, which was organized by the Socialist Party at the turn of the century) gave the left wingers their own branches, but in Cleveland it refused to transfer three left-wing leaders to the new branch that I had joined. They were entitled to all the benefits of the Workmen's Circle, but they were not permitted to participate in meetings. After a while the three members appealed to the National Executive Committee. Two of the applications were approved, but the third one was held up because the applicant had been charged with collecting money for a recent defense fund and not giving an accounting of it.

When the Cleveland District Committee of the Workmen's Circle, to which I was a delegate, decided to hear his case, I defended this man. The night of the meeting he gave me duplicates of receipts that he said he had given to people from whom he had collected money. At the meeting one of the right wingers pointed out that some of the receipts had been written the night before when they should have been dated a year prior to that. The committee decided against his application.

After the meeting one of the right wingers asked me, "Max, you knew that he was wrong because you yourself brought charges against him in the past on the same subject. I know that you are an honest man. How could you defend him?"

At that time, I was not thinking too much about right and wrong. I did what was expected of me as left winger. I am sorry now that I had.

After a few months, this man went to another city where he was appointed city director of the International Workers Order (a new organization, under Communist control, composed of the left-wing branches, which had broken away from the Workmen's Circle).

On another occasion, the delegates of several branches of the Cleveland International Workers Order voted against sending the district secretary to a conference in New York. He then took the floor and said that the national office had appointed him delegate (which was against the wishes of the membership) and he was going. A couple of months later, he asked permission of the district committee to take a vacation. They refused, but he took the vacation anyway. While he was away, the treasurer of the district committee opened his mail and found a check for $80 from the national office. He did not know what it was for, so he wrote to New York to inquire about it. They replied that it was for an organizational fund and that they had been sending $80 a month for a year. This had never been reported to the district committee.

The treasurer was an honest and gentle man. He did not want to hurt or insult anybody, but he could not stand pilfering from the organization. He told me about the checks and said that he knew I would do the right thing.

I preferred charges against the district secretary at a meeting of our branch, of which the secretary and treasurer were also members. I was called before an investigatory committee. Its members asked me how I knew about the checks. I told them what I knew, and if they wanted to be sure that what I said was true, they should examine the books of the district committee.

The findings of the investigatory committee were that I had made false charges against an active member and an officer of the IWO. I was fined $25, and was asked to write letters to the national office and the *Morning Freiheit*, a Jewish left-wing paper, apologizing for the "mistake" I had made. I refused to pay the $25 or to send the letters.

The treasurer could not swallow this ruling. Later, somebody preferred charges against the secretary in the Communist Party of Cleveland. The CP appointed three people to investigate these charges. They found him guilty of mishandling money and recommended that he be dismissed as district secretary.

You might have expected that the officers of my branch would have recalled the fine against me, but they never did. The branch refused to accept my dues, and I lost my membership (I then rejoined the Workmen's Circle). Many of my friends advised me to appeal to the executive committee of the IWO in New York. I felt that this would be useless and that such an appeal would result in the secretary's favor. Several months later this man was appointed district secretary in another city. This was the justice handed out by the Communist Party.

In 1926, I was asked to attend the Trade Union Educational League (TUEL) Conference in New York. At this conference a dual union resolution was proposed and passed, although the official policy of the group had been to oppose dual unions and to work within the existing AFL locals (The name of the group was changed in 1928 to Trade Union Unity League and the policy to one of support of dual unions).

I had been an active member of the AFL for fifteen years and felt that any split in the ranks of labor would be disastrous (I supported the C.I.O. when it was founded because it organized unorganized workers and did not compete with the AFL). I asked the chairman to explain his reasoning for this dual-union resolution, and the only sense I could make out of his long answer was that it would provide jobs for party functionaries.

You don't resign from the Communist Party; you must be expelled. Back in Cleveland, I did nothing to carry out this resolution. Eventually, the Cleveland Communist Party summoned me before its executive committee. The meeting was for a day that I usually set aside to collect money for the IWO. That day I collected money as usual, and even went to the homes of some of the executive committee members. The next time I was summoned, I went. I was asked why I had not appeared last time and why I did nothing to carry out the resolution of the TUEL convention. I told them that on the day I was to appear, I had to wash my baby's dirty diapers.

You don't resign from the Communist Party; you must be expelled.

I was expelled from the party.

I never missed a meeting of my Paperhangers local except for the brief period that I resigned from the union to become a contractor.

Very often, I would write articles for the *Cleveland Citizen*, the Cleveland Federation of Labor paper, criticizing the actions of the leaders of the Painters' Union and calling for more union democracy. This did not endear me to the leaders. Once I was called upon the council floor to be censured for my articles. They threatened to have them stopped, but this they could not do because Max Hayes, the editor, was on my side. Mr. Hayes, a well-known socialist who ran against Samuel Gompers for the Presidency of the AFL in 1912, encouraged me in my writing and said that he would print my articles so long as I told the truth.

There were a number of nationality clubs such as the Jewish painters club, the Italians, the Russians, etc. These clubs had nothing to do with the Painters' Union officially, but they were interested in jobs for their members, and they entered into arrangements so that their members were given first choice.

In 1920 we kicked out Fred Miller and his gang from the leadership of the Painters' Union in Cleveland. One high member of his group once stood at the top of the stairs of a Painters' hall and hit anyone who came up the stairs who had disagreed with him with a baseball bat. Many men were hurt by this drunken man, but he wasn't arrested,

The new leadership under Brother Cook, in time, became just as bad. There was an unofficial slugger at our meetings by the name of Moses Donnelly. Whenever anyone got out of line, Moses would attack him with the vilest language and at times would use physical violence as a weapon.

In all of my years in the union, I was never attacked physically, and I had the freedom to say what I wanted. I suppose this was because I would not attack any individual and never used any of the adjectives, which most of the leaders used in their criticism.

When Brother Charles Smith, the Cleveland Federation of Labor secretary, died in 1927, the Painters District Council No. 6 suggested that all delegates attend his funeral. At the next meeting the Council voted a day's wages to each of the 32 delegates for attending Brother Smith's funeral. As one of the delegates from my local, I voted against this resolution, because I knew that only the Painters secretary and two business agents from the Council had attended the funeral, and since they were paid officers of the union, no time was lost. The resolution passed over my objections.

Several days later, I asked for the floor at a meeting of Local 867, the largest painters' local in Cleveland. The president of the local, who was also a member of the Council, refused to recognize me, but some of the members insisted that I be given the privilege of the floor. I informed the membership that the Council had voted $320 out of the treasury for itself for not attending the funeral of Brother Smith, and I asked them to instruct their delegates to the Council to recall this resolution. This they did overwhelmingly.

At the next meeting of my local, the members also approved of my dissenting vote and instructed the other delegates to vote for a recall of the resolution. One of the delegates said on the side that he wished I had been shot in Leavenworth eight years ago.

About twenty-seven of the thirty-two Council delegates voted at the next meeting for a recall, and they all agreed that I should have been shot.

I had to pay the price of my stand, however. When I came up for reelection, I was defeated. The argument used against me went like this, "You see Max Sandin? He didn't want to take money for himself. Do you think he's going to work against the contractors in getting raises and benefits for you?" Many of the workers bit this.

The very fact that the political machine was against me was enough to ensure my defeat. The average worker was afraid to do anything that would put him out of favor with the business agent, because it was upon him that the worker depended for jobs.

Paperhanging, like painting, is a seasonal trade. I could only work when the weather was good and that was about seven months a year. The wages I made were not enough to carry us for the other five months. And for a family of four, it was four times as difficult.

The first four months of the season, I had to work to pay off the debts of the last months of the slack season. There were times when we owed the grocer and butcher each over a hundred dollars and were ashamed to ask for more credit. Many a winter we would have starved if they and the chicken man had not come to us and said: "Mr. and Mrs. Sandin, we are not afraid for you. We know that you are honest people and that you will pay us." We always paid them in full.

When Irene was about twelve years old, she wanted a bicycle quite badly. We went to the Sears, Roebuck store where the salesman assured us there would be no problem in charging one. She picked one out and we were told that it would be delivered in four or five days. Irene told all the kids on the street that we had bought her a new bicycle. Several days later we received a letter stating that our credit was not in perfect condition and that they could not deliver the bicycle. Try to imagine how this girl felt. Something like a defeated candidate for the Presidency.

During Coolidge's "prosperity" there were millions of families that had little to eat or money to call a doctor if someone was sick or for fuel or medicine. During this period, the Employers Association in Cleveland succeeded in breaking a collective agreement with the Painters, Decorators, and Paperhangers Union. A large number of craftsmen were working in open-shop conditions, and in the small towns it was much worse. Our work was seasonal, and the bosses played worker against worker with such devices as piecework and the speed-up.

I ran for delegate to the 1928 conventions in Ohio of the Painters' Union, Building Trades Council, and Federation of Labor, on a platform that called for an organizational drive to bring about one hundred percent union conditions in the trade and to better our position in the Building Trades Council; a 40-hour five-day week; collective agreements by the building trades with employers that expired on the same date; more democracy in the unions so that the membership would have the final say in wage negotiations, grievances, strikes, and other actions that directly involved their interests; the formation of a labor party that would be controlled by the workers; and, most importantly of all, legislation for a state unemployment fund.

My calling for a state unemployment fund drew the fire of many in the Painters' Union. I was called a radical, Bolshevik, Communist, and many other names. Nevertheless, my fellow workers elected me delegate, and I received a check in the amount of $175 for expenses.

The machine, however, could not tolerate my election, so they found an old by-law that said five members-in-good-standing could call a special meeting. When the meeting was called, only those members that could be relied on were notified. I was charged with being a contractor and therefore ineligible to be a delegate to the conventions. I denied the charge and demanded that they prove it. The business agents said they had no proof but had heard rumors to that effect.

I knew that it was impossible to win in such a packed meeting, so I told them "You know that I was legally elected and that I have the check for expenses in my pocket. Nobody can stop me from going, but I will resign as delegate on one condition — that Brother Kirchner go in my place." I knew that I could trust Brother Kirchner to do what I would do at the conventions. The membership agreed to this and the bosses were prevented from naming a hand-picked man.

The Communist-sponsored Organization for Jewish Colonization in Russia (ICOR) was founded to collect money for agricultural machinery and supplies needed for a farm. We set up an organization whose members pledged a certain amount each month. I was one of the active members soliciting members and pledges. In May 1932 a membership drive was inaugurated with the prize being a trip to Biro-Bidjan, where the Jewish autonomous state was proclaimed. An ICOR circular proclaimed "that Max Sandin brought in the most members." However, the trip to Biro-Bidjan was enjoyed by someone else, as I was not a Party member.

CHAPTER FIFTEEN

Unemployment Insurance

Max Sandin circa 1930s. Photo courtesy of Deborah Tenenbaum.

It is not easy for those of you who are young to comprehend the misery of The Depression [1929 to 1939]. Think how it would be if you suddenly lost your job, your savings were wiped out, your children were screaming for lack of food, and were shivering because they were cold; and to top this off, there was no unemployment insurance to help you out until you found another job. This is the predicament millions of workers found themselves in when the depression gripped this country, and the predicament they remained in for a number of years.

Those tears in the eyes of the workers who insisted on waiting in line when the banks closed were real. They were hoping beyond hope. What could they do? Starve? Kill themselves? Many did. Accept charity? Most of us were forced to, but it was degrading for a man who was capable and willing to work for his own support.

It is amazing to look back upon those days, and realize that we had to fight for unemployment insurance, a right which we take for granted today. The American Federation of Labor and its leader, William Green, were opposed to it. Ever since the days of Samuel Gompers, the higher-ups in the AFL had denounced unemployment insurance as "the dole," as a "barnacle" on the labor movement.

A growing number of us felt that a man had a right to work and that if he is out of work through no fault of his own, he and his family should not be penalized. We formed the American Federation of Labor Members' League Favoring Unemployment Insurance. In Cleveland, a group of us in the Painters' Union organized under the leadership of Trent Lengo, one of the business agents. We were active in educational work in the union and did our best to win over the Federation of Labor to the cause of unemployment insurance.

At first, the AFL threatened us with expulsion. At its Vancouver convention the Federation reaffirmed its traditional opposition to unemployment insurance, but the utter despair and increasing militancy of the workers, who were forcing their local and state organizations to come out for such workers' security, caused the executive committee of the AFL to change its stand in 1933.

Meanwhile, millions of workers were forced to go to charity to keep their children alive and reasonably healthy. It wasn't easy to ask for help or something to eat when we were treated as if we were something other than human. My union had always contributed to the Community Fund, and, for that matter, the thousands of dollars contributed by large concerns really came from the sweat of the workers, but when we went to a "charitable" organization, we were told "You can work for 25 cents an hour," and, in effect, scab on union labor.

The schemes were numerous. Our high-salaried citizens spent thousands of dollars to advertise their generosity to the unemployed, and to our children who were being starved and thrown out onto the streets. They placed a large milk bottle in the public square in Cleveland for everyone to see. But that was a bluff to fool the hungry workers. How many children were helped by that fund? My brother-in-law had been out of work for eight months. He, my sister, and their five underfed children were not given milk or bread by these people.

The man-a-block people would send men to work on a city block at scandalously low rates. While ostensibly helping the working man, they were causing him to scab on union labor and were thereby breaking down the bargaining position of the unions and the standard of living of the American worker. At the same time, they were providing cheap labor for the rich landlords.

A member of my local union received a letter from the Independent Order of Foresters on March 14, 1932, with the following application form. "I am able and experienced in the following and willing to work for 50 cents an hour temporarily: Carpenter, plumbing, electrical, mason, painting, paperhanging, auto repair, auto cleaning, general house cleaning."

All of these trades were organized by the AFL, and if he had accepted, he would have been scabbing and working against his own interests."

The *Cleveland Press* of October 21, 1932, carried the following article:

> Charity organizations and the city must act soon to halt their present practices or there will not be enough police in the country to protect them when the crowd breaks loose.

> Harry McLaughlin, president of the Cleveland Federation of Labor, made this assertion before delegates to the Federation last night. McLaughlin said he was not a Communist and has fought their activities in every direction, but that hungry men will not be reasoned with. He called on charitable organizations to favor pay in money for work.

> McLaughlin charged that men who worked two days in the park and
> are supposed to get $8.80 for it, get a grocery slip for $2.85. He asked
> where the rest of the money goes and held that such practice took
> honesty and independence away from every individual.
>
> Labor will never subscribe to any plan which turns over to some charity
> group the decision of who shall or who shall not work.

The Associated Charites would write to those receiving groceries: "You must
come to work for three days and we will raise your order for one dollar more of
groceries. Come ready with your lunch at 7 a.m. . . ." It wasn't enough that we had
enriched this country with our labor, but we were forced to labor for bread, which
was being provided by us through gasoline taxes and the tax-supported Recon-
struction Finance Corporation. If we refused to do forced labor, our relief was cut
off or cut down by these "charitable" organizations. There were many instances in
which social workers cut down a worker's relief order if they learned that he had
been paying union dues.

In the depths of the depression, the Unemployed Councils were formed to take
direct action against evictions and to demand more relief and unemployment insurance. I joined the Unemployed Councils because they were made up of the workers
themselves. The Communists did not officially sponsor the councils, but there was
no doubt they were on top in them. The Councils were made up of people of many
political complexions, because hunger knows no bounds politically.

We would have people to our house for coffee and cake and sometimes a
piece of herring. That is all we could afford. We would discuss our mutual problems and take up a small collection to help those who needed it most. When
families were evicted, we would protest in the streets and sometimes move that
family back in. (Many landlords were afraid to leave apartments vacant, because
people in their desperation for warmth or food would chop down doors or
remove the plumbing.)

On November 30, 1932, I was one of several hundred delegates who left
Cleveland for a hunger march on Washington sponsored by the Unemployed Councils. We stopped at Akron, Beaver Falls, Youngstown, Pittsburgh,
Uniontown, and Cumberland, Maryland, on our way. In Pittsburgh, the city
administration supplied us with about 1,500 gallons of free gas for our cars and

trucks. The people of the towns we passed through greeted and cheered us, but the police made sure that we moved on.

We arrived in Washington on December 4th. An army of 12,000 federal and city police greeted us and imprisoned us in the street at the end of New York Avenue. We were not allowed to go out of this police circle and no one was permitted inside of it to see us. There were 3,000 delegates there representing the unemployed workers of this country. They had come to petition Congress for unemployment insurance and $50 for winter relief.

On Monday we had a demonstration of all the hunger marchers confined to the police circle. After the demonstration we had an open-air mass meeting. The police threw stones and bottles at us in order to provoke a fight, but our leaders told us not to play the policemen's game. Thanks to their coolness, bloodshed was prevented. That evening the chief of police gave us a permit to march.

On Tuesday morning, we started our demonstration through the streets of Washington. We marched four abreast, with two policemen on each side. The papers reported that several hundred thousand people were on the streets watching us. We stopped about two blocks from the Capitol and sent delegations with our demands to see Mr. Curtis, the Vice-President, and Mr. Garner, the Speaker of the House.[8]

When we left Washington, with slogans "Tax the rich and feed the poor," "They will stand on their heads, they will stand on their feet, the hunger marchers can't be beat," "Black and white unite and fight," we knew that the fight for Unemployment Insurance had only begun and that we would have a long and ferocious struggle ahead with our bosses in the shops and factories and with our lawmakers in the legislatures.

While the charities were practicing forced labor among the unemployed and breaking down the labor unions, unethical practices were being employed in their fundraising techniques. Here are some quotes from Theodore Dreiser's *Tragic America*:

> In May, 1931, an investigation of Mayor Mackey's Committee for
> Relief of the Poor and Unemployed, with Charles B. Helms as director,
> was started by the City Council of Philadelphia and the District

---

[8] *Editors' note: See online 1-minute video http://recordsofrights.org/records/367/hunger-march-video*

Attorney. It was brought out that "high pressure" telephone solicitors of the Mayor's Committee used the name of a Philadelphia hospital to secure funds, also the name of the American Legion. They even used blind men as solicitors. These promoters managing charity shows contracted with a hospital and nurses' alumni to put on a benefit performance and give the hospital the "gross receipts" less ten percent commission to the promoter. Each year, as a result of the performance, this promoter has given the hospital sums ranging from $350 to $450, with his alleged ten percent deducted. He has actually collected $5,000 to $10,000 on each performance. It was revealed that during his four years of so-called charitable service he has netted about $30,000, while the hospital received less than $1,500. ...Yet Charles B. Helms, the director, said that he had permission from the Mayor only to sell tickets for benefit shows and secure advertising in programs and nothing else.

Yet according to the true American standard as it operates today, Helm's agreement with the Philadelphia Mayor was a 20 percent commission to the promoter. But, in practice, they took even more. An audit of the books showed that 64 cents of every dollar solicited went to the promoters.

...But now look at this astonishing budget of funds set aside by the Rescue Mission in New York for the year ending in November, 1930:
　　$15,000 for office expenses
　　$15,000 for advertising
　　$25,000 for salaries
　　$44,000 for radio broadcasting for funds
and only $5,000 to feed the unemployed! And all in the name of God and charity, both of which, of course, should be overthrown.

The charity rolls were growing daily. On September 21, 1933, President Roosevelt said that there were 3,500,000 American families on relief rolls. Jay Franklin wrote in the September 1933 *New Outlook*, "I am familiar with accurate figures of these Americans who are entirely dependent upon dole in the United States, but I'm not at liberty to cite it. It is a figure which would surprise and shock the public for the dole-supported population thereby represented is greater than the entire population of many foreign nations."

The social workers were overwhelmed by the number of persons forced out of work, and they proved themselves entirely inadequate in handling the situation.

Alexander Bevilacqua said in the same issue of *New Outlook*:

> The job of prevention is one that entails something deeper than just the application of high-sounding terminology; the job of rehabilitation is something more involved than merely providing undignified and transitory "jobless labor"; the job of readjustment is one that calls for more sympathy and understanding than what is known by supercilious workers grown independent because they have become political untouchables. In many large cities ordinary policemen used to make the investigations to determine whether or not a family was deservedly on the charity list. Without benefit of pedagogic psychological terms, they went colloquially to the heart of the problem and got results. Today our highly trained workers with a halo of ethics about their heads and the backing of persons overawed by their colloquially and oftentimes incomprehensible phraseology, have made a tragic mess out of the business of administering relief.

This crisis was in its fourth year. Charity handouts were not enough to go around to all. We needed unemployment insurance desperately. We increased our work in the American Federation of Labor Membership League for Unemployment Insurance. I wrote scores of letters to the *Cleveland Citizen* criticizing the present system and calling for unemployment insurance. One year, I was a delegate to a hearing before the Ohio state legislature on unemployment insurance for the AFL Membership League.

Sometime in October 1933, I received my weekly grocery order from the Cuyahoga County Relief Administration (CCRA) with a 20 percent cut. The accompanying letter explained: "The budget of the Cuyahoga County Relief Administration for October is not large enough to continue giving relief on our present standards. Attempts have been made to secure supplementary money, but without success. We find that it will be necessary to decrease everyone's grocery order the last week of month. November orders, if funds can be secured, will return to the previous amounts you were receiving." The letter was signed by Stockton Raymond, the director of the CCRA.

My reply to Mr. Raymond, which was printed in the *Citizen*, was, in part,

> You are receiving a salary of $6,000 a year; that is about $125 a week. You cut my relief to $5.57 for a family of four to live seven days on.

But you did not cut your own salary to $100 a week on account that the October budget is not large enough to continue giving relief on our "present standard."

In the *Cleveland Press*, Sept. 30, an item stated: "$1,165,500 awarded county for relief." Also, "The money is largely from Federal coffers," and "the administration also adopted a resolution to RAISE the collective pay of relief workers by a total of $6,000. The increase was made on the recommendation of a committee appointed to study salary conditions of the works and conforms to the standard prescribed by the State Relief Commission."

How come that my weekly grocery order is cut 20 percent because the County Relief had not enough money, and at the same time you gave a raise in wages to the steadily employed social workers of $6,000 of the unemployed relief money?

In the same issue of the *Cleveland Press* an article in capital letters stated: "Cleveland Food Costs Mounting. Prices Higher U.S. Averages on Seven Commodities, Lower on Six."

That means another cut in my weekly grocery order, doesn't it?

Which day in the week shall my family go hungry?

Now, Mr. Stockton Raymond, director, Cuyahoga County Relief Administration, you shall know that I am determined that neither I nor my family will go hungry, not even one day. I will do anything to provide my family with food, clothing, shelter, heat and light. Jail, prison or the chair won't stop me.

I am out of work against my will and I am getting poor relief against my will. I don't want charity. I and all of the unemployed workers who are getting relief (charity) know that the present scheme (unemployed relief) is only to "tax the poor and to feed the rich."

No! We do not want your scheme (charity). We demand unemployed insurance, so we will have enough to eat every day. And we don't need $6,000-a-year men to dish out meatless and breadless days to our children.

We demand unemployment insurance to be paid by the government and the bosses and managed by the workers.

In March 1934 the Civilian Works Administration (CWA) sent me to work on the Woodland School. I had worked previously for the CWA on the Mount Pleasant School, but between the two jobs I had a week's vacation from the CWA, without pay.

I had been a steward (the person who is responsible for the rights of the painters on a job) on the Mt. Pleasant job for about ten weeks, so the men on the new job also elected me steward with the consent and satisfaction of the Painters District Council.

When we started to build our scaffolds, some of the men called my attention to several planks that were cracked. I ordered the foreman to take them off of the job. I also found some tools that were in dangerous condition and called that fact to the attention of Mr. R. C. Neilson, the supervisor. He said, "Goddamn it. It's none of your business."

About ten minutes later, Mr. Neilson came back and asked, "Who in the hell gave you the authority to talk in the name of these painters? I am going to fire you as an agitator."

I told him that the painters had elected me as their steward, and I showed him a paper signed by all 33 painters giving me the right to speak for them. He walked away saying "You won't stay on this job very long."

About a week later, I was sandpapering a clothes closet, when a painter came to me and told me that five painters were ordered to paint one closet and were given only three brushes to do it with. He began to help me. The other painter who had no brush to work with also came over to help.

Suddenly Mr. Neilson screamed, "I am going to fire all of you. There are six hundred hungry men waiting for your jobs. You must work here."

How could we work when there were no tools with which to work? Was it useful work when 26 painters were told to paint four closets for the day when two painters could do it in one day? What was the sense of painting walls when the next day the plaster would be removed to fix something?

Later that day, Mr. Metzger, the business agent, asked me what kind of trouble there was. I told him there was no trouble. He said that Mr. Neilson had called him and wanted him to come over immediately. As the business agent and Mr. Neilson were talking, I went over to them and asked Mr. Metzger about the standing of the men on the job. Mr. Neilson grabbed me by the arm crying "You are fired. Get out of here," and he kicked me.

I was given a note to see a member of the school board the next day. When I appeared, I was told that I was fired from the CWA job because there was "considerable unnecessary agitation on the job, which was very much disliked by all concerned."

The Painters District Council decided to support me and take action to have me restored to the job. Mr. Metzer and I went to see someone at the CWA. He transferred the case to someone else to whom we gave a signed statement of the facts in the case. He promised to investigate as soon as possible. I never heard from him.

I was fired from the CWA job because I had done my duty as a duly elected steward in protecting the lives of the painters on that job.

I was one of twelve unemployed workers arrested on June 27, 1934, at the CCRA Miles Avenue branch. We went there as a committee to see the assistant secretary with whom we had an appointment. As we walked up the stairs to his office we were met by a guard and a policeman. We told them of our appointment. Instead of permitting us to enter, we were placed under arrest and taken downstairs to a waiting police wagon.

On July 6th, we were brought up before Police Judge Stacel on charges of disorderly assemblage. He released us with the comment: "These men and women are not guilty of anything except that they are hungry. I think you social workers should not waste your time by bringing them into court. They are punished enough by having to come to ask for bread."

I was arrested again on July 13th at the same office of the CCRA when I went there with six others to demand a new mattress for a crippled boy. When we appeared before Judge Stacel, whose attitude toward us had changed, he characterized us as "dangerous persons" and placed us under $500 bond. I later spent three days in the workhouse for my petition.

Two members of the Unemployed Councils had been killed at another office of the CCRA. The police charged that one man had grabbed a policeman's gun and shot a woman demonstrator in the crossfire. A policeman killed the man. As a result of this incident, the police posted more guards at relief offices.

The United States government finally made it possible for most of the states to pass unemployment insurance acts by the passage of the Social Security Act in 1935, which imposed a payroll tax on all employers having eight or more employees in "covered" employment. As an inducement, 90 percent of this tax could be offset if the employer paid unemployment taxes under a state law meeting certain standards. The act also provided federal money to the states for the administration of these funds. Every state, the District of Columbia, Hawaii, and Alaska, enacted unemployment insurance laws by July 1937.

A long, hard battle in changing the climate of opinion in this country had been won. What we got was not the best. It did not provide full security of wages for 52 weeks of the year, but it provided an adequate basis for the worker to maintain his dignity when he was forced out of work for no reason of his own. Also, unemployment insurance payments could not be denied if the worker refused to accept a new job due directly to a strike, walkout or other labor dispute, at wages, hours, or conditions for substantially less than conditions for similar work in that locality, or in which he would be required to join a company union or resign from or refrain from joining any bona fide labor organization.

Chapter Sixteen

Two Jobs

I n 1936, the president of the Cleveland Painters District Council was sent to prison for taking a bribe from the builders. Much racketeering was going on in this administration, which had become worse than the old Miller crowd.

A new movement, which called itself the Progressives, was formed to oust the present corrupt regime. I became active in this movement. Some of us overlooked the fact that its leader was a half-communist, half-antisemite and that some of the nationality painters' clubs had joined together, because we wanted to rid the union of gangsterism.

After a bitter fight, arrests, hospitalizations, and court trials, twenty-three of the Progressive groups, including myself, were expelled from the union. Our fight was successful, however, and we were reinstated. The trials were dropped and wounds were healed.

For a while, the administration consisted of rank-and-file members who were inexperienced in politics. We elected a new day secretary and new business agents.

There were some mistakes and misdeeds, but this administration ushered in a new era and is still at the head of the Painters' Union in Cleveland today.

When the Progressives took over the administration, they discovered that work on a large new apartment building was not being done by a legitimate contractor but by a union man who was not getting enough money for the job to pay the union scale. The union took over this job and sent painters directly to the builder. Because it was winter, and many painters were out of work, the union ruled that the jobs should be rotated.

I was out of work at that time and had just run out of coal. A friend of mine mentioned my predicament at a meeting of his Jewish painters' club. Brother Weinberg suggested a collection to "get Max some coal." Fifteen dollars was raised. I accepted the money but I knew that Weinberg had meant it as an insult. Weinberg and the leaders of the club had never liked me. Back during the Hunger March on Washington, I had asked this club if I could represent them. They refused and I had to go to another Jewish painters' club, where the rank-and-file liked me, to be elected a delegate.

My friend told me: "Max, why don't you go up to the painters' club. They are sending men out on Mr. Aronoff's building on Warrensville Road (the one that had been taken over by the union)?"

Because of the pressure of some of my friends, this club decided to give me a week's work on the Warrensville job. I did not know why it was the club's business, which was a private group, and not the union's.

When I went up to the club rooms to see a friend, I saw brother Weinberg giving cards to several of the men. A friend of mine asked me if I had a card. I said no. He said that I could not work without a card from Weinberg.

The next day the foreman on the job told the builder that Max, the shoemaker, was coming to work. The builder asked the foreman why the Painters' Union was sending shoemakers to work on his building. He said he was not paying him to have his shoes fixed. The foreman got wet pants.

When I reported to work, the foreman asked me for my card, I showed him my union card.

"No, not that card."

"I have no other card," I told the foreman.

He said that I could not work there then.

When the steward came around, I told him that the foreman did not recognize my union card. He asked the foreman why be wouldn't let me work. The foreman said that I did not have a card like the other Jewish boys had. The steward said he did not know what he was talking about but that I should be put to work until the business agent came around to straighten the matter out. The foreman refused.

When the business agent arrived, I told him that the foreman would not recognize my union card but wanted another card before he would let me work. He asked the foreman what card he meant. At that point the foremen pulled out a handful of business cards which belonged to the business agent and which said "O.K. Materse." That was his name.

"Where did you get those cards?" he wanted to know.

The foreman became red in the face and said that Weinberg had told him not to let anyone work without that card.

At this point, I took out a card like the ones in the foreman's hands and showed it to him.

"But why didn't you give it to me?"

"Because it is my property," I replied. "I paid for it." The business agent asked me where I bought it and for how much. I told him that I had paid $10 for the card; where I bought it, I would tell somewhere else.

A friend had actually given me the card. The reason I did not show it to the foreman but to the business agent was that this was racketeering. Weinberg had no right to send union men onto the job, and I would have been an accomplice to this dirty business if I had used that business card.

I was put to work, and I found out that many of the painters had been on the job ever since it began in spite of the union rule of rotating the jobs. There were a number of men from different painters' clubs, including the officers of the Jewish painters' club. Only the uninformed dues-paying members were working in rotation, and they had to pay for these extra graft cards.

At the end of the week, the builder asked me to come back the next week. When I did, the foreman asked me what I was doing there. I asked him why he and many of his comrades had been working since the beginning. I worked a while longer and the club racketeering was broken.

In September 1937, I was waiting in the union office with several dozen painters for job openings. The day secretary called out that there was a job for about three or four hours. Did anyone want it? No one answered. One of the men said, "Why don't you ask Sandin?" I was a Jew and this man believed a Jew would do anything, so he suggested me. I decided to accept.

A man drove me over to the new veterans' hospital which was being constructed. I was to prime some siding. Because of the time it took to get there and the papers I had to fill out, I only had a half hour of actual painting. He asked me to come back the next day.

As I finishing the siding, I noticed someone watching me. He came over and introduced himself as the president of a painting company, which had the contract for the hospital job. He said that I looked like a steady worker and that if I wanted, I could stay on. There was about eighteen months work; I accepted gladly.

When the men who had been in the union office waiting for a good job learned of this, they were sore. According the union rules, the first man in the job is the steward. He cannot be fired by the contractor, and he must be the last man on the job. One of the painters asked me if I could take him on the job. I told him that I would ask the contractor when another job opened up.

1 worked there by myself five days a week for four months. Sometime in January, the contractor asked me to go to Akron, Ohio, to prime some sash and frames in a wood mill for the hospital. I agreed and asked him if he could use another man. He agreed and I told Mr. Campbell, the man who had asked for a job in the union office.

Campbell stayed on and others joined us at the hospital. I took this man to work and home again every day in my car.

My wife and I decided to send our daughter to college from the money I earned on this job.

I began to hear rumors from some of the painters that Campbell wanted to push me off the job so he could become steward. Mr. Campbell, who had been a member of the old guard in the Painters' Union, which we progressives had ousted, accomplished this by circulating a petition among G.I.s from the first World War demanding that I, a conscientious objector, be thrown off this veteran's hospital job.

As I was putting on my overalls one day in May 1938, the superintendent came over to me and said: "You son-of-a-bitch! Get off of this government property." I asked why, but before I could finish, he said that if I didn't leave right then, he would call the sheriff. I told him I would wait for my boss, but he said I couldn't wait there.

So, I left his property and waited in no man's land for my painting contractor. When he arrived, he told me that he had nothing against me, but that he could not do anything for me because he was in business and not in politics. He told me that Mr. Campbell had caused all the trouble.

I went to the union office where I found out that the union had received a letter from the veteran's administration asking that it not cause any trouble on a veteran's job on account of a conscientious objector "who would not defend his country."

Several painters told me in the union hall that Campbell had been laid off the following week for loafing.

Part Four:
Another War

CHAPTER SEVENTEEN

Refusal to Register

Once again, the people of the world were being dragged into war. Governments covered up the inhumanity of war with cloaks of self-righteous idealism and preyed upon their citizens with such terms as Patriotism, Honor, and God. The constant beating of drums and inflamed oratory drowned out any pleas for sanity. The fact that millions of human beings would be slaughtered or permanently maimed wasn't even considered.

The workers of the world were split into many quarreling factions, and the overwhelming majority of them supported the war, having substituted loyalty to state for loyalty to class and to humanity. Nowhere was there in evidence any resolutions condemning war as strongly and as unequivocally as had the anti-war resolution of the Socialist Party in 1917.

I was driving home from Columbus after a visit with my son when I heard on the car radio that Pearl Harbor had been bombed. This raid provided an excellent excuse for the United States to join in the slaughter. I knew that in some way or another I would be affected. I could not keep quiet about something that I believed to be a crime against humanity. Maybe I would wind up in prison again.

It was not until five months later, that I was to be directly confronted. On April 27, 1942, I was required to register for the draft, along with all the other men between the ages of 45 and 65. I was then 53 years old.

I had written previously to Selective Service Director Lewis Hershey and Attorney General Francis Biddle, informing them that I could not comply with the conscription law.

As far as I know, only 20 men in that age group openly refused to register, although there were indications that many thousands more never showed up at their draft boards.

Of these 20, 16 are known to me. Among them were Harold Studley Gray, Howard W. Moore, and Evan Thomas, who were in Fort Riley and the United States Disciplinary Barracks at Fort Leavenworth with me during World War I. Julius Eichel, who was confined to the U.S.D.B. at Fort Jay and other military prisons during World War I, and Ammon Hennacy, who was held in Atlanta Penitentiary then as a civilian prisoner, also refused to register.

The other non-registrants on April 27th were A. J. Muste, Frank Olmstead, Edward C. M. Richards, Ralph Templin, Norris E. Woodbury, Walcott Cutler, Peter Beike, Walter Bullen (who was 47 days away from becoming 65), Richard B. Gregg, and Walther Longstreth.

We were assured by the government and our friends that it was unlikely we would be drafted, that this was just a "census," and that at the most we would have to change jobs, but in spite of this assurance, and the threat of a prison sentence and heavy fine if we failed to report, we could not keep silent about the immorality of war. This was our way of speaking out.

Several days after the 27th, I received a "Notice (to registrant) of Suspected Delinquency" from Local Board No. 31 for Cuyahoga County, which said "According to information in possession of this Local Board, you have failed to perform the duty, or duties, imposed upon you under the selective service law as specified below. To present yourself for, and to submit to, registration. You are therefore directed to report, by mail, telegraph, or in person, at your own expense, to this Local Board, on or before 7:00 pm, on the 4th day of May, 1942. Failure to report on or before the day and hour specified is an offense punishable by fine or imprisonment, or both. M. Hausman, Clerk of Local Board."

I did not answer this notice. I expected to be arrested, but no one came for me.

Shortly after the letter from the local board, I was paid a visit by the clerk of the board. One afternoon when I came home from work, my wife told me of the clerk's presence in the front room. After changing my paint-stained clothing and cleaning up, I went into the living room to greet the lady clerk. She told me that she had come to ask me to sign the registration papers.

When I told her that I would not sign any document that had anything to do with the war, she explained that I might be sentenced to five years in prison and receive a $5,000 fine.

"The government's threatening me with prison or a fine will not change my stand against war," I told her.

My wife and daughter were crying and on the verge of fainting. "See," the lady clerk lectured me, "Your family is suffering because you are a stubborn man. You know very well that you won't be drafted. Who will take care of your wife and children when you are sent to prison?"

I tried to explain to her that no one benefits from wars except those who have an interest in them like the munitions manufacturers. The common people are only killed or maimed. I could remain home silently with my wife and daughter, but what good would I be to them if I were miserable with myself? I said that I could not register, not because I was stubborn or selfish, but because it was the only sane course I could take, and it was a step toward making this a world in which my wife and children would be truly safe.

I did not hear from the government again until several months later. I had been working all that year on a steel job in Painesville, Ohio, for the Austin Company of Cleveland. One day I was called into the office. The supervisor told me that an FBI agent was in the next room and had given him a registration card for me to sign, I told the supervisor that I was a conscientious objector to war and could not give my consent to it by signing the card, he said that I could not work there anymore. It was a good job, and I was the fourth man on the job and had seniority rights, but I had to sacrifice it for what I believed in.

The Conscientious Objector, a newspaper for C.O.s, printed the story and I was very happy to receive the following letter of encouragement and offer of help from a fellow non-registrant who had been with me in Fort Riley and the U.S.D.B. at Fort Leavenworth.

Cherry Valley, N.Y.
October 6, 1942

I have been intending to write you for a long time. As a matter of fact, ever since Julius Eichel came up to see me last spring and gave me your address. But pressure of work here on my farm has forced me to neglect most of my correspondence.

It was especially gratifying to learn of your stand again in this war, and I know it required a great deal of that old Sandin courage to make such a decision because of family responsibilities which a large number of the old group evidently felt was sufficient reason for registering.

I have just learned from the last issue of *The Conscientious Objector* that you have lost your position because of your failure to register. Such things entail hardships, and if it would mean anything to you, I should be glad to have you and your wife, whom I should be glad to meet, pay me a visit for an indefinite period. We should also be glad to welcome your daughter. I presume that your son is working but if not, we could accommodate him also. As long as the government doesn't interfere further in our lives we would, at least, have plenty to eat and be comfortable.

Julius, Esther and Seymour, their son, were here for a few weeks this summer and we enjoyed having them. Julius ran up only for week-ends. I believe they enjoyed their stay here and Esther was great help to mother.

Both my parents are old. Father is a semi-invalid but mother is in good health but not as efficient, of course, as she used to be and I am sure Mrs. Sandin could help her do the cooking and housework for us. I don't know whether you would like the isolation of farm life or not, but I have found it about as secure a place to be as any. I mean by that that one can make a simple living and have a greater measure of independence than in the city in times like these.

Let me hear from you and remember me to any of the boys whom you may happen to run across.

With every best wish and warmest personal regards, I am
As ever,
Howard W. Moore
(Twenty-one years later, I thank you again, Howard Moore.)

After losing my job, I decided to go to New York for a vacation. I stopped off in Buffalo on my way and found work for several weeks. But back in Cleveland, I found it increasingly difficult to get work because of my stand against the war. It was nearing the end of the painting season, and because my family was quite upset about my stand, I decided to go west for a while. About October 15, I boarded a bus for Los Angeles, along the way stopping in Tucson, Arizona. The first morning I found work through the Painters' Union.

So, I went to look for a room. Seeing a sign "Room for Rent," I asked the landlady, "Can I rent your room?" She responded, "What sickness do you have?" I told her, "I am not sick." She replied, "I'm sorry, you cannot have the room," and closed the door. I was puzzled why she refused to let me have the room since I wasn't sick.

"What sickness do you have?"

About three streets farther I see another "Room for Rent" sign. I asked the lady who came onto the porch, "Can I rent your room?" And she asked, "What sickness do you have?" I told her, "I am not sick." To my surprise she said "You can't have this room if you have no sickness." I asked her, "Please tell me, why don't you want to rent me the room if I'm not sick? You are the second lady who refuses to rent me a room for the same reason?" She replied, "Most people come here with a sickness and we rent the rooms with board. So, we have to know the sickness of each person in order to know which table to sit them at eating time." I rented a room without board but this experience was worthwhile.[9]

I worked in Tucson six weeks. When that job was completed, 16 of us were laid off. We went over to the union office where there were not many able painters. About noon the business agent in the office called out, "I have a telegram from the

[9] *Editors' note: Arizona had been a key destination for those with tuberculosis; Tucson itself had a number of sanatoriums.*

Santa Fe Painters' local asking for ten men. Who wants to go?" Five painters raised their hands and I was one of them.

The business agent explained the conditions of the job: one day fare for each man, seven days a week, and ten hours a day. The wage was $1.25 an hour as in Tucson, Saturday and Sunday double that. Also, for painters who work 30 days, they will get a day's pay to go back. One of the painters had a car. It was about 500 miles through Arizona wilderness but we made it in one day. Sunday, we put on our overalls getting ready to work. We waited two hours but the foreman did not show up.

Monday morning the foreman came on the job with five painters from Denver. He did not want to put us to work because the Denver scale was $1. We demanded that he live up to the conditions as stated in the telegram. Well, he put us to work but at 4:15 fired all four of us, giving us a pink slip and told us to go to the office for pay. We had a heated argument with him but he drove away.

Then the next morning, Tuesday, we put on our overalls and started to put up the scaffolds. When the foreman arrived about 8:30, he fired us again, but we kept up moving planks and ladders. He tried to stop us by force but he was not strong enough. By 9 am the supervisor came over and asked, "What's going on here?" We explained about the telegram with its conditions and that the Tucson local sent us out here to work. The foreman said that after he sent the telegram to Tucson, he decided to go to Denver where the union scale is only $1 a day.

The supervisor said that he thinks that the Tucson men are right and that they shall get paid for all the time they worked or lost through no fault of their own. So, we got paid double time for Saturday and Sunday, and for Monday, Tuesday, and Wednesday — seven days equivalent at $1.25 an hour — totaling $87.50. We returned to Tucson.

Two days later I went to work for Mr. Bridges a contractor from Phoenix. He sent us to a project in Ajo, Arizona, population 6,000 with 18 saloons, 12 churches, one library (open Saturday afternoon for four hours and Wednesday from 6 to 8 pm), and an open pit copper mine. I worked there five weeks.

After that, I headed for Los Angeles. When I arrived, I went the union office where I met many Cleveland painters, including a friend of mine from

Cincinnati who I hadn't seen in about 20 years. He told me that he is a foreman on a job and that if I want to go to work, he will take me on his job. The next day I was working with him.

I was told at the Painters' Union in Los Angeles that the Jewish painters hung out in a stationery store on DeSoto Avenue and Brooklyn Street. As I was approaching the store, I was surprised to hear someone say, "Hello, Max!"

I didn't recognize him.

"I'm Louis Enhoren from Cincinnati. Don't you remember I stayed at your house one night in 1927, and you got me into the Painters' Union?"

"Now I know who you are," I said, happy to meet a friend.

Louis was from Dvinsk. I had seen him there last when he was about four years old. When he came to this country, he had looked me up, and I had been pleased to have him as a guest.

"Are you looking for work?" he asked me. "I am the foreman of a school painting job and would be happy to have you come to work with me tomorrow." I accepted his offer, found a room near him, and met several of my old friends from Cleveland.

Several weeks later, I met Mr. Seleznik, who had been a left-wing union politician in Cleveland. He had been one of those who had done their best to have me thrown off the job on Mr. Aronoff's building in 1937, because I would not follow the "line." He told me that he was out of a job and had no money to pay his rent. Besides, his wife and children were hungry.

I called my friend Louis and asked him if he could put a friend of mine on the job. He said that he couldn't but that he would ask the contractor tomorrow if there were any other jobs. I asked him if it would be all right if I took the afternoon off and let my friend work in my place. He did not object. The next day the contractor heard about what I had done and found a job for Mr. Seleznik, who worked for him for six months.

So, I paid with a good deed for a bad deed and am glad.

Meanwhile, I was wondering what I could do, an individual, to make my protest effective against the war. One day I was reading about Henry David Thoreau's refusal to pay taxes to support the Mexican War, in "Essay on Civil Disobedience," and found encouragement in the following words:

> Cast your whole vote, not a strip of paper merely, but your whole influence. A minority is powerless while it conforms to the majority; it is not even a minority then; but it is irresistible when it clogs by its whole weight. If the alternative is to keep all just men in prison, or give up war and slavery, the State will not hesitate which to choose. If a thousand men were not to pay their tax-bills this year, that would not be a violent and bloody measure, as it would be to pay them, and to enable the State to commit violence and shed innocent blood.... If the injustice ... is of such a nature that it requires you to be the agent of injustice to another, then, I say, break the law. Let your life be a counter friction to stop the machine. What I have to do is to see, at any rate, that I do not lend myself to the wrong which I condemn.

I decided to follow Thoreau's example of not paying taxes, but first I decided to check with an American Civil Liberties Union attorney in Los Angeles. He advised me that to refuse to pay taxes was a very dangerous thing to do and that I might have to go to prison.

I also wrote to the War Resisters League in New York and received the following reply from another fellow non-registrant and former prison colleague, Evan Thomas:

> The War Resisters League
> Room 414, 2 Stone Street
> New York, New York
> April 14, 1943
>
> Dear Max:
>
> Thank you for your letter from Los Angeles, I enjoyed hearing of your visits with the Molokans, and I am very much interested in your stand with regard to income tax. Maybe you are right about that, but I cannot at the moment see any clear-cut way of protesting against the war through refusal to pay taxes. If one refuses taxes, the government can conscript whatever possessions one has and I do not feel like going to prison over that particular issue. So far as principle is concerned, I believe that community has the right to conscript for the benefit of all. I admit that taxes at present are not being used in that way and no doubt a good case can be made for refusal to pay.

Best of wishes as always,
Sincerely yours,
Evan W. Thomas

After much deliberation, I decided to send in an income tax return with the following words written on it: "As a conscientious objector, I refuse to pay income tax — not to help war directly." I sent the letter by registered mail and asked for return receipt. Next day, I went to work with the good feeling that I had done something I wanted to do.

I was happy to learn from the April, 1943, *The Conscientious Objector* that another C.O. — Mrs. Marie Nelson of New Rochelle, New York — had refused to pay income tax that year and that several others had paid under protest.

The business agent told me that there was a job opening at Camp Pendleton, the naval base near San Diego. I discovered that the Austin Company, which had fired me from the Painesville job, was constructing a hospital there, so I decided to apply for a job with them.

On the application form I noted that I had not registered for the draft. The personnel man did not say anything as he read over the form, but told me to return the next day. I was surprised when they put me to work.

After working on the job for several weeks, someone told me that I was wanted in the office. Waiting for me were two FBI men who said they had been notified about my notation of not registering for the draft. They asked me many questions about my life and beliefs. About 4:30, I told them that I thought we should quit with the rest of the workers. As I left the room, one of the agents pointed to a file quite thick and said that it was my record from the first day I had entered this country.

I waited to be fired as I had been from the Painesville job, but apparently the Austin Company needed painters badly because I was kept on.

One day I had just climbed upon a scaffold to go to work when the foreman came in and announced that the government had frozen the job and that no one could quit. I climbed down from the scaffold and started to take off my overalls.

"Max, what are you doing?"

I told the foreman that I was quitting.

"Didn't you hear me say that the job is frozen and no one can quit?"

"That's why I am quitting."

I asked him for my pay.

About three-quarters of an hour later, he came back from the office with my pay and gave it to me. He said I could quit if I wanted to or I could go back to work. Having established my right to do what I wanted; I went back to work. The men congratulated me and shook my hand. At quitting time, I was surprised that my stand had become known all over the job.

Waiting to be arrested was a difficult thing. I knew that someday the government would send its agents for me, and I wanted to get it over with. In order to force the government to make its move, I always indicated on job application forms that I had not registered for the draft.

In San Francisco, where I went next, I noted my refusal on my application form for a job at city hall. I was not arrested, and I did not get the job. Next, I applied for a job in the shipyards. Surely, I would expect them to notify the government. I did not get the job, and I was not arrested. After working a week in San Francisco, I decided to return to Cleveland, where the painting season had begun.

CHAPTER EIGHTEEN

Jail

S hortly after I returned to Cleveland, and began working on a housing project on Babbitt Road, I received the following letter from the United States attorney's office in Cleveland:

June 24, 1943
Max Sandin
3925 East 142 Street
Cleveland Ohio

Dear Sir:

We wish to inform you that it has come to our attention that you have not registered under the Selective Service Act of 1940.

We hereby notify you that you must register with Local Board No. 31, 13409 Kinsman Road, by July 3, 1943.

Please notify this office when this has been accomplished.

Very truly yours,
Don C. Miller

United States Attorney
by Francis X. Fighan
Asst U.S. Attorney

Early in July, I received another letter from Mr. Miller:

Dear Sir:

Referring to our letter of June 24 1943, we wish to call your attention to Section 613-16 of the Selective Service Regulations which states in parts:

"If the registrant refuses to sign the registration card…the registrar shall sign such registrant's name, followed by the word Registrar, beneath the name of such registrant, and the act of the registrar in so doing shall have the same force and effect as if such registrant had signed the registration card and such registrant shall thereby be registered."

In event that you, Mr. Sandin, refuse to present yourself and submit to registration under Section 613-16, a complaint will be issued and you will be taken into custody of the United States Marshal. Unless you comply with the law by July 15, 1943, we have no alternative but to carry out our duties in this matter.

1942 draft registration card

We are instructing Local board No. 31, Cleveland, to inform us whether or not you have appeared by July 15, 1943.

Don C. Miller

U. S. Attorney

I ignored this letter too.

The day of reckoning came on August 13, 1943. When I came home from work, my wife told me that two government men had been looking for me. While we were talking, the agents came back to the house. When I answered the door, one of them asked if I was Max Sandin. I said yes, and he handed me a warrant for my arrest. The other agent handcuffed me, and I was led to their car.

On the way to the county jail. I was told that I would have to stay in jail until Monday morning, when I would be given a hearing. They had been looking for me since noon, they said, and now it was too late to arrange for bail, because the United States District Attorney's office was closed.

When we arrived at the Cuyahoga County Jail — unlike the District Attorney's office, the jail was open for business, 24 hours a day — I was handed over to a "welcome" committee, consisting of two deputy sheriffs. They "invited" me to empty my pockets and to sign a paper giving them permission to open all my mail. I did the former but refused to sign away my privacy at that point. Next, I was "asked" to take my weekly Friday night shower, which I did.

After these preliminaries were over, I was taken to a suite reserved for federal prisoners only. My memories of Camp Funston, Fort Riley, and Fort Leavenworth came back. It was the same cage with the same iron bars on the windows and doors. The bull-pen consisted of tables and chairs where the prisoners were permitted to play cards or checkers, or to read. The prisoners were provided with bibles, but most of them used their bibles for gin-rummy scores. At night we were divided up and placed in smaller cells.

Of the thirty-odd prisoners on that floor, I learned that another was also a conscientious objector. He was a member of the Jehovah's Witnesses — a sect which will not participate in man's wars but will only fight in the final battle of Armageddon on the side of God. I tried to speak with him, but he wouldn't answer me.

I have always been ambivalent about working in prison. One gets bored with long, drawn-out hours of nothing to do, so working helps to relieve the tedium. Also, one learned what is going on in the jail by circulating among the other prisoners. But I also feel that since I did not ask to be put in jail, I should not be asked to work while in jail.

I wiped the dishes Saturday morning and mopped the floor, but I decided not to work after that for as long as I was in jail.

When the deputy sheriff woke me the next morning, I told him of my decision. He threatened to give me a cold shower in bed. I got up but told him that I would not work and I would not go to breakfast. As punishment, I was transferred to the sixth floor, where the rough guys were kept.

At noontime, I refused my food. I told the other prisoners, who were curious about my not eating, that I was going on a hunger strike for the length of time I was in jail. They said I was a damn fool.

In the afternoon, their strong-armed leader announced menacingly that I was to be tried at a kangaroo court. The prisoners gathered eagerly around a table and the leader, acting as prosecutor, started the proceeding.

"The trial of the god-damn conscientious objector, Max Sandin, is now open."

He read a newspaper clipping about my arrest, my leaving Russia, being sentenced to be shot, and refusing to register for the present slaughter. When he had finished, the prisoners broke into applause and shook my hand. However, the prosecutor continued: "Charge number two. A new prisoner has broken into our club. What do you honorable citizens of Cuyahoga County Jail think we should do with this intruder?"

After an ominous silence, one of the prisoners proposed that I be fined three dollars for the cigarette and stamp fund. "All in favor of this motion," the prose-cutor-turned-judge said, "raise your hands." The resolution passed unanimously.

When I told them that I had no money to pay the fine, the jury showed mercy and gave me from 60 to 90 days to pay. However, they warned me that if I wanted to appeal the decision, I would have to pay the fine first.

The next morning, Monday, August 16th, I was handcuffed to another prisoner and taken to a courtroom for arraignment before United States Commissioner B. D. Nicola. I was charged with willfully disobeying the

President's order to register on April 27, 1942, for the draft of all men between the ages of 45 and 65. When the Commissioner asked me if I would register now, I said, "No, no, I am a free man in a free country. War is only organized wholesale slaughter and ..." A marshal placed his hand over my mouth to prevent me from going on.

The Commissioner asked me how I plead. When I refused to answer, he pleaded not guilty for me and placed me under $1,500 bail. I told him I would not furnish any bail, so he said he would have to send me back to jail.

At this point, two men with beards stood up in the courtroom. One of them asked for permission to speak, which was granted. "We do not know Mr. Sandin," he said, "but when we read about his arrest in the newspapers, our Quaker Church instructed us to come to this hearing to provide bail for him, if he needs it." I asked for permission to speak, which was also granted.

I said to the men, "I thank you very much for your good deed, but as an atheist I cannot accept help from a religious group."

The Commissioner then really got mad and raised ball to $2,000 in cash.

A deputy handcuffed me, and I was led back to jail.

Before I had been arrested, I told my daughter, who was going to New York to visit her aunt, to stop in to see Evan Thomas at the War Resisters League to give him my greetings. When she did, Evan told her of my arrest and that the WRL, a non-religious pacifist group, had made arrangements with a bonding company in Cleveland for my release.

I continued my hunger strike. When a friend, Max Ratnoff, brought me a box of candy, I gave it to my fellow prisoners. They thanked me and their leader announced: "Max has paid his fine with sweetness." The prisoners applauded.

The inmates were constantly complaining about the bad state of the food and coffee. I was glad that I wasn't eating. On Thursday, the food must have been unusually bad because the prisoners swore and spat all day long. One of them got the idea that if I could go on a hunger strike for five days they could also. All the prisoners shouted agreement. They threw their plates and cups through the iron bars and turned over the soup and coffee pails. When the sheriff arrived, a spokesman said: "We refuse to eat this god-damn swill. We're going on a hunger strike, like the god-damn conscientious objector."

The leaders of the demonstration were taken away and locked in solitary cells. The sheriff said he would look into the matter the next day.

The prisoners continued their swearing throughout the night. But no one ate the next morning. Finally, one of them began to blame me for all their problems and their hunger. I reminded them that they were the ones who had said the meat was horsemeat, as some of the guards had told them, and that the coffee was like melted snow. I suggested that they could probably improve the food by writing a letter to the newspapers about the stinking bread and smelly meat.

"That's all fine," someone shouted. "But who in the hell will get this letter to the outside?" I volunteered, because I knew that I would be called before the Commissioner fairly soon. "Besides," I said, "what can they do to me? I'm already in jail. All they can do is throw me out."

On Monday morning, I was handcuffed and brought up before Commissioner Nicola. As I entered the courtroom I handed the prisoners' letter to Mr. Miller, the United States Attorney. Mr. Miller read it and handed it to the sheriff, with the comment that it was a hot potato.

The sheriff asked me why I had not signed it. I said that I had not eaten for nine days. Some of my friends in the courtroom heard me and started to applaud. The Commissioner silenced them and said that his courtroom was not a circus.

Commissioner Nicola informed me that a $2,000 bond had been posted for me and that I was free until my trial. I went off with my friends to a restaurant, where we spent several hours talking about my jail experience. I had a piece of toast and a delicious glass of milk.

I gave a copy of the prisoners' letter of grievances to a Cleveland *Plain Dealer* reporter, but the letter was never published.

On August 20th, Holton wrote one of his Holtograms in the *Cleveland Citizen* about my arrest:

> According to the *Plain Dealer* of August 17th, in 1918 Max Sandin was a Conscientious Objector, and in May 1942 when men up to 65 years were ordered to register, he refused to do so, was sent to jail, and has been there ever since. We used to think Max was a good scout. Well do I remember when he was a delegate to the Cleveland Federation of Labor from the Painters' Union, Local 128. He was a hard worker for

Unemployment Insurance. We owe a big debt to Max, Chris, Pat Burns and others for their efforts in behalf of Unemployment Insurance. Pioneers, Oh "Pioneers." Max suffers as a martyr to his convictions. He was, and is bitterly opposed to WAR, bloodshed and mass murder as he called it. In spite of his views on war we who fought for Unemployment Insurance when it was unpopular to do so, respect and love him.

When I returned to work on the Babbitt Road job, I learned that several of the men had drawn up a petition asking the foreman to fire me because I had not registered for the draft. About eighteen of six hundred men had signed the petition, and the foreman had refused to fire me. Many men shook my hand and said they were glad that I was back.

In 1955, I met Mr. Kravitch, one of the men who had circulated the petition to have me fired. When I reminded him of this, he said that he didn't remember circulating any petition but that he notified the U.S. Attorney that I had not registered. He said that he was sorry.

The work season had begun in Florida, but I did not want to risk losing the $2,000, which was put up for my bail. I asked the advice of an old friend, William K. Thomas, who is now a judge. Sometime in October, I received the following reply him:

Dear Max:

I am told by Francis Feighan that you will not be prosecuted. It may take a little while for the charge to be formally dismissed. However, if you hear nothing within the next month, call me again and we will contact Feighan and see that the formal dismissal is put through...

Yours sincerely,
W.K. Thomas

He had advised me to see the bonding company about leaving town. When I did, the manager told me to contact Mr. Miller, the district attorney. This I did, and when I told Mr. Miller that I was going to Florida, he did not answer me. I waited for a few minutes and when he still did not answer me, I left his office.

Several days later, I was on a bus for Florida. I never heard about my case again. I worked in Miami for six weeks and after a short vacation, I returned to Cleveland on February 1, 1944.

Part Five:
War Bound

Max Sandin with his daughter Irene circa 1940s. Photo courtesy of Deborah Tenenbaum.

CHAPTER NINETEEN

Taxes and War

On March 15, 1944, I continued to protest the war effort by refusing to pay income taxes. I wrote across the top of a return, as I had the previous year, the following words: "As a conscientious objector, I refuse to pay income tax, not to help war directly." I signed my name and address — but filled in no other information — and mailed it to the Internal Revenue Service.

Sometime after that I was called in for an interview with an officer of the IRS. The collector told me that he had received the form with the notation of nonpayment but that he could not excuse me from paying income taxes. "Every citizen who earns enough has to pay them. That is the law."

I told him that I had not supported war in the past and that I could not condone the slaughter that was now going on. I certainly was not going to pay taxes when most of the money would be used for this insanity.

When he realized he was getting nowhere with me, he tried another tact.

"Why don't you pay me the 25 percent you say goes for constructive purposes, such as for health, schools, etc."

"If I paid that 25 percent," I answered, "75 percent of it would go for war. The government does not differentiate or allot tax money in that way."

> *Exasperated with me, he stormed, "Do you think you will get away with violating a federal law?" "No, but I can't go against my convictions. I am ready, but unwilling, to take any punishment you have in the book. But I won't violate my conscience."*

Exasperated with me, he stormed, "Do you think you will get away with violating a federal law?"

"No, but I can't go against my convictions. I am ready, but unwilling, to take any punishment you have in the book. But I won't violate my conscience."

In subsequent years, I was pursued frequently by agents of the IRS. Sometimes, when I would leave for work, two men would follow me in a car. Often, I would drive around for hours with them on my tail, and then return home, instead of going to work. When I tried taking a bus or streetcar, one of the men would get on with me, or they would be waiting when I got off.

I tried to avoid them by parking my car several blocks away and walking through several backyards to it. One day, however, a neighbor warned me not to cut through his yard anymore. The agents had told him that I was running away from them. He said that he would shoot me if he caught me trespassing on his property. The tax men told him that he may do it.

I once arranged for a contractor to pay me every day after work. After the third week, he said: "Max, I cannot use you anymore. The federal men were here today and asked for your pay. They said I would be arrested for helping you not to pay your taxes. I don't want to have any trouble on the job."

I took a small job — a day's work — removing wallpaper from a room for $20. When I left my house in the morning, I thought I saw somebody following me. At noontime, when I asked the landlady for an advance for lunch (although I had lunch money), she gave me $20 for the entire job. When I finished, the woman told me that the federal agents had visited her and asked for my pay. They were angry, she said, when she told them that I had been paid in advance.

I was laid off another job because my employer thought it was bad for his business to have the tax men looking through his books.

That is the way it went. Sometimes the tax men were successful in collecting money and in frightening my employers. Other times they were not. Any time they collected money from my jobs, I feel that my conscience is clear. The money that I earned was small compared with the money the government spent in paying men to trail me, and no bullets are being bought with my money.

The money that I earned was small compared with the money the government spent in paying men to trail me, and no bullets are being bought with my money.

In 1955 they garnished three weeks' pay for about $325. And in 1954 over $115. I did not get any receipt from the tax men. I do not care for money. Never in the 45 years (in this country) did I have a bank book, savings account, stocks or bonds but I am glad that my lot is to fight for myself and the rest of the people to free the world from further wars and child killing.

I learned that there were a few other individuals who had arrived at the position of not paying war taxes. Ammon Hennacy, an agricultural worker in Arizona, who had been in jail during both wars, had been refusing income taxes for years. Finally, in 1948, he was told that a court order would be issued to collect his taxes. Ammon would quit whenever he learned that his wages were going to be attached. He worked at many jobs where he was paid at the end of the day. When the agents became persistent, he asked and received his pay before he started to work.

Mary Bacon Mason, a musician and music teacher from Newton Center, Massachusetts, began refusing in 1946, and said in a statement to the IRS: "The only possible defense for any people is friendship and mutual help. That is real defense. I will pay my full tax if I can be assured it will be used for aid to suffering people anywhere. But rather than use, make, or pay others to use the sinews of war,

I will accept prison or worse." Referring to World War II, she said: "I paid a share in that cost, and I am guilty of burning people alive in Germany and Japan. I ask humanity's forgiveness."

Valerie Riggs of Cambridge, Massachusetts, began in 1944 to pay only that portion of her tax bill which corresponded to the nonmilitary figure. Her husband Francis Riggs, joined her in 1947.

Walter Gormly, a self-employed consultant engineer from Mt. Vernon, Iowa, was the first confronted by the tax men in 1944 when he was in prison for conscientious objection. When asked why he had refused to pay, he said: "My money would be used mostly for crimes against peace.... And I don't want to pay to keep myself in prison."

Ernest Bromley, a Methodist minister in Bath, North Carolina, began his tax refusal in February 1942, when he refused to buy the required automobile windshield "defense tax stamp," because it would be direct financing of the war. He subsequently served 60 days in the county jail for refusing to pay $7.09, which he contributed to the Methodist Commission for Overseas Relief. The first time he made enough money to owe income taxes, in 1944, he refused to pay them.

Marion Coddington (who later became Mrs. Ernest Bromley) tried unsuccessfully to get her employer, the pacifist Fellowship of Reconciliation, not to withhold taxes from her salary, so she resigned from the Fellowship. She wrote to the IRS in 1947: "This country did not turn to peace at the end of World War II, but instead sought to protect and expand an American empire. I want to dissociate myself as completely as possible from these tragic, suicidal and evil policies, and to do all I can to convince my fellow citizens that we must completely renounce the way of war and violence."

In the spring of 1948, several hundred radical pacifists, including myself, got together in Chicago to explore revolutionary methods of nonviolence. This was the beginning of Peacemakers. We came out of that conference pledged to nonregistration to the draft, refusal to do war work, and a number of us, to refuse taxes for war. A committee, consisting of Ernest Bromley, Marion Coddington, Walter Gormly, Valerie Riggs, Caroline Urie, and Ralph Templin was set up to further nonpayment of taxes.

Caroline Urie, who lived in Yellow Springs, Ohio, and later in Cleveland, was a veteran social worker and had been an associate of Jane Addams. She was the widow of a naval medical officer. In 1948, she began her tax refusal by holding back 34.6% of her tax. In a letter to President Truman, she wrote: "Now that the atomic bomb has reduced to a final criminal absurdity the whole war system, leading quite possibly to the liquidation of human society, and has involved the United States in the shame and guilt of having been first to exploit its criminal possibilities, I have come to the conclusion that — as a Christian, Quaker, religious and conscientious objector to the whole institution of organized war — I must henceforth refuse to contribute to it in any way I can avoid.... In the present case, I can no longer acquiesce in the action of my government in taxing me to maintain armed forces for the political purposes of war."

Ralph Templin of Cedarville, Ohio, who had been a missionary in India for 15 years before the Methodist mission board expelled him for his sympathies with the Gandhian nonviolent movement for independence, began his tax refusal while working as a part-time professor at Central State Teachers College in Wilberforce, Ohio. He wrote one year:

> Our Federal government has become little more than a war machine. Even the value of that 'little' is negated by the total war motivation, which we once believed was possible only for a totalitarian society. For this reason, I am as much opposed to the totalitarian nature of the withholding aspect of the income tax as I am against war or the war uses to which so large a percent of the money is put. The former (the compulsory tax method) is the necessary means to the latter (the making of war) in a nation which no longer takes the people into consideration in the conduct of the foreign affairs. Conscription and war-levy seem now as much the way of this nation as they were formerly of the most extreme European tyranny which we originally resisted in our colonial history.

The hundreds or so people who came to our tax refusal movement were from all walks of life — there were ministers, teachers, librarians, housepainters, lawyers, doctors, carpenters, salesmen, religious people, atheists, world government advocates, anarchists, etc., but we had one thing in common: we were determined to do our best to prevent another war or another tragedy like Hiroshima or Nagasaki.

As Rev. A. J. Muste, the national chairman of Peacemakers, and a tax refuser, said to the press in 1949: "The greatest possible evil today is that of atomic and biological war. We must use every possible means, including civil disobedience, to stop the possibility of our country waging war."

In 1948, the Internal Revenue Service took out a lien against all my property and rights to property. Several weeks later, I signed a contract for a painting job at a place where there had been a fire. I had arranged to receive $50 before I started and so much at the end of each day. At the end of the second day, I was told by the man who paid me that he had received an insurance check for the fire, and it would take several days for it to clear at the bank. When I asked him again at the end of the fourth day, he told me that he had been visited by the IRS men, and he showed me a receipt for the amount of money I was to receive. There was nothing I could do. The government had extracted $121.08 from this man.

On March 8, 1949, a Notice of Levy was issued, against my employer at that time. It read:

> You are further notified that all property, rights to property, moneys, credits, and/or bank deposits now in your possession and belonging to the aforesaid Max Sandin and all sums of money owing from you to the said Max Sandin are hereby seized and levied upon for the payment of the aforesaid tax, together with penalties and interest, and demand is hereby made upon you for the sum of two thousand eight hundred sixteen dollars ($2,816.74) of the amount now owing from you to the said Max Sandin or for such lesser sum as you may be indebted to him, to be applied in payment of the said tax liability.

This amount supposedly covered delinquent taxes and interest for the years 1942, 1943, and 1944.

The IRS was full of surprises. That year, I received a tax refund for $63. I had sent in a withholding statement with my notation of nonpayment written across it, and apparently the accountants who figure from those slips arrived at this refund in spite of the $2,816.74 which they said I owed.

Chapter Twenty

The Tax
Men Strike

Bald Man's Stand Against Paying Income Taxes
Leads to Constant Battles With Revenue Men

CLEVELAND — (AP) — The little bald man said he wouldn't pay his income tax this year, just as he has refused to pay it since 1943 when he decided Uncle Sam used tax money to pay for wars and killing.

There was a fleck of white paint under Max Sandin's ear as he sat in the newspaper office to make his annual declaration. It was literally an earmark of his trade, housepainting.

In his hand he carried a news release headed: "43 refuse to pay federal income tax," and it was from the 'Tax Refusal Committee of Peacemakers."

Actually the number now is 42, because Mrs. Caroline F. Urie, a naval officer's widow, died last week.

Sandin was a personal friend and neighbor in suburban Lyndhurst of Mrs. Urie, who made headlines by withholding 75 per cent of her income tax payment. She figured that percentage went for military expenditures, so she paid it to charities instead of to the government.

"I won't pay even 25 per cent," said Sandin, "because they would take 75 per cent of that and use it for war purposes."

Sandin's stand for peace has, of course got him into his own small private war with the Internal Revenue collectors. Outnumbered, he has lost a few battles, but his foe is fighting on a long front and is unwilling to spend the time, patience or money to achieve total victory

that would net about $3000 in tax money. Also, the opposing high command doesn't want Sandin as a prisoner, and in the skirmishes the house-painter has certain tactical advantages.

When Sandin works steadily for the same contractor, the Internal Revenue officers latch onto his pay check before he painting jobs, the collectors have to wait outside his home, board the bus with him and give notice to the homeowner that Uncle Sam, not Sandin will collect for the paint job.

Peace from this private war with the tax collectors is just around the corner for Sandin, who is 65. He plans to retire next summer and write a book

entitled "Political War Objector."

In it he will tell how he has opposed war since World War I when he was sentenced to die for refusing to bear arms but was saved from a firing squad by President Woodrow Wilson's last-minute reprieve. And he will tell how he was jailed in 1943 for refusal to register for the draft in World War II.

"I oppose war politically, not religiously," he explained. "Who am I to say that I'm the only person whose conscience objects to war?"

Sandin's retirement income won't be a matter of much concern to the Internal Revenue Department. It will come mostly from social security.

"I paid those taxes," he said.

Athens Messenger, *Athens, OH, April 11, 1955*

J im Otsuka, while a student at Earlham College, became the first tax refuser in modern days to be criminally prosecuted. He had refused to pay 29 percent of his tax, or $4.50.

At one point in the hearing before the United States District Court in Indianapolis on August 19, 1949, the judge said to Jim: "How would you like to go back where you came from?" (Jim was born in the United States of Japanese ancestry.) The judge demanded that he give information as to the source and amounts of his earnings, when Jim hesitated, the judge threatened him with contempt of court. After Jim gave the information, the judge asked him: "And now are you going to pay the tax?"

Otsuka still refused and the judge gave him until September 1st to pay, or to face "serious consequences."

On September 1st, part of Jim Otsuka's statement to the court read as follows: "I have faith in the ultimate goodness of all men, groups and nations, for this goodness exists now, and I believe that I can serve in making it grow by my participation in the way of nonviolence. I am convinced that I am following the right path, guided by divine providence, in helping to apply love and mutual aid between individuals and among peoples of every race, creed and color."

The judge asked him what this meant, and in the course of explaining it Jim said that he had written it before entering prison in World War II.

"What? You weren't a soldier, were you?"

"No. I was in prison as a conscientious objector."

"And that didn't teach you anything?"

"Only that I am even more convinced of this stand."

"You are placed in custody of the attorney general, sentenced to 90 days in jail, a fine of $100, and costs."

As Jim was being led out, the judge turned to this lawyer and said, "I don't see how you can represent him. It is a terrible thing for a young fellow to take all the advantages of living here and then to refuse to pay his taxes."

Because Jim Otsuka refused to pay the fine, he had to spend another 30 days in prison. On December 29th, he was taken before a United States commissioner who ordered him imprisoned indefinitely if he refused to pay the fine. Because of the stir this decision caused around the country, Jim was released unconditionally on January 16, 1950. The government had been unsuccessful in collecting $4.50 in war taxes and in forcing a young man to go against his deepest beliefs.

On March 15th, Jim Otsuka went to Oak Ridge, Tennessee, where he took an early morning commuter bus into a restricted area of the atomic bomb plant. He passed out leaflets urging the discontinuance of work on the bomb. At noon, while in the custody of the FBI, he burned seven-tenths of a dollar bill, as a symbol of what is happening to every tax dollar.

On November 15, 1953, I started to work for a large painting firm, Louis Spector & Son, employing 40 to 50 painters. I believe my work was satisfactory to them and, for my part, I had no grievances or complaints against the boss, foremen, or any of my fellow workers.

However, several times during the 30 months I was working there the IRS garnished my pay for about $700, in addition to the regular withholding tax. I continued working there because it was the first steady job I had had in all my years as painter, and I was now 65 years old.

One day in the second week of April 1956, my employer came over to me and said, "Max, I would like that you should quit." I told him that I have no reason to quit. I liked him, his wife, and all my fellow painters on this job. Finally, my boss, who had been harassed constantly by the tax men, said, "Max, please look for another job. It hurts me when the tax men take away your hard-earned money."

I was out of work for about six weeks. Whenever I ask for a job and tell them my name, the answer is, "We do not want any trouble." What next? I do not know.

Another tax lien was filed against me on November 9, 1956, for the collection of $379.08, which the IRS said I owed for 1954. I continued to receive pre-summons notices, summonses to appear, final notices before seizure, etc. I would visit the tax men occasionally, when they requested, and reiterate my stand against war.

In the spring of 1958, several conscientious men set out for the Eniwetok bomb-testing area in the Pacific in a sloop called the *Golden Rule*. They had decided to sail into the United States' test area to challenge the men conducting the nuclear bomb tests. They believed that by placing their bodies beneath the bomb, they could get these men to realize what they were doing — how they were poisoning the sea and atmosphere, how they were preparing for another and most horrible war. Their protest was under the auspices of the Nonviolent Action Against Nuclear Weapons Committee which had committed civil disobedience the year before at the nuclear test grounds in Nevada. (This committee later became the Committee for Nonviolent Action.)

Meanwhile, an ad hoc committee initiated by Peacemakers got together to plan a Walk for Peace from Philadelphia to the United Nations and simultaneously from New Haven to the United Nations in support of the men of the *Golden Rule*.

When the walks reached the United Nations a week later, the number of demonstrators had grown to about a thousand, making this the largest pacifist demonstration in the United States, up to that point, since the thirties. [ED. NOTE: *Max's notes are not clear but it's likely that he joined some part of the walk to the UN.*]

At the same time, about 1,250 persons had walked from Aldermaston, the site of Britain's Atomic Weapons Research establishment, 50 miles to London's Trafalgar Square, where over 5,000 persons participated, in what was to be the first of a series of annual massive demonstrations during the Easter season.

The *Golden Rule* men were stopped by the United States Coast Guard a few miles out from Honolulu. As a result of their protest, Albert Bigelow, a former Housing Commissioner of the State of Massachusetts, William Huntington, an architect, Jim Peck, a veteran pacifist actionist and author, George Willoughby, chairman of the Central Committee for Conscientious Objectors, and Orion Sherwood, a school teacher, were sentenced to 60 days in jail.

Upon my return to Cleveland, I found a summons ordering me to appear before the Internal Revenue Service. When I appeared, two men grilled me as to where I worked, how much money I made, etc. I refused to answer most of their questions, and after about three hours of questioning they threatened to have men posted at my house to follow me to work (this would be nothing new), to sell my car, my furniture, and my house (which I didn't have), to attach my Social Security checks — in short, to stop me from living. I told them I could not cooperate with them, because I would not do anything that might eventually hurt human beings anywhere in the world.

In early September, the IRS served a summons on Rev. Maurice McCrackin, pastor of a combined Presbyterian and Episcopalian Church in Cincinnati, Ohio, to appear before it with records and sources of his earnings and assets. Rev. McCrackin, who began refusing taxes in 1949, wrote back that he would not be present and that he was unwilling to make any payments, or to give any information which could help in a collection.

On September 12th, Federal marshals came and took him, without his cooperation, to a hearing before a United States Commissioner. He said later, "If I had walked, I would have felt I was in prison, but in not walking, I felt that I was free."

When the court tried to obtain an attorney for him, he refused, saying that God was his advocate. They tried to get him to agree to a date for a hearing, but he said: "According to the summons, you say you will bring the body. The body is here. I am trying to follow my conscience, and you fellows will have to do what your conscience leads you to do."

The Commissioner asked him if he would sign a bond for his release, but Rev. McCrackin refused. "I am not going to sign anything. You brought me here, and what happens to me physically is beyond my control — but you can't control my spirit." Rev. McCrackin was placed in a cell in the marshal's office. Four hours later the door was opened and he went home. The commissioner had set a hearing for September 26th, but Rev. McCrackin did not appear on that date.

On November 7th, the federal men came for Maurice McCrackin. He refused to cooperate and they had to carry him into the United States District Court. He refused to stand or to step to the bar to plead. He told the judge that he would cooperate with making a plea where it did not involve him in cooperating with the government's attempt to force him to pay for war.

"This refusal to step to the bar is more serious than your failure to answer the summons," the judge lectured. "I give you one last chance to step up here and plead. If you don't, you may spend the rest of your life in a mental institution."

He was released on November 20th after being subjected to a mental test to see whether he was capable of standing trial. On November 24th, he was carried back into the courtroom.

When asked to make a plea, Maurice McCrackin said: "I have only this to say: that the government cease making materials to destroy the world and that it respects the conscience of those who do not want to support these efforts with their money. This is my only plea." The judge had him carried back to jail, until such time as he had purged himself of contempt.

On December 12th, he was sentenced to six months in prison and a fine for "neglecting to appear and testify and to produce books, records and memoranda."

The judge showed his ignorance and prejudice in saying:

> You have admitted giving your donations to the Fellowship of Reconciliation and the Peacemakers instead of paying taxes. These groups are notorious and have overwhelming Soviet sympathies. We won't go into whether you are a card-carrying Communist or not.... Tax money is to provide the United States of America with a means of defending itself against Communist Russia. Even this morning the newspaper accounts were rattling the bones of war. They say they will take America without firing a shot. And here is Mr. McCrackin saying he will not give taxes to the government because it is evil. I don't know of a more pious way to be called a traitor than that.

Maurice McCrackin's contention that because the building of ghastly instruments of death has the support of law, and the forced collection of money to manufacture these things also has the support of law, the court cannot be anything but a partner with the IRS when it serves as an agency to enforce the law, was well borne out.

Rev. McCrackin's adherence to the Commandment, "Thou shalt not kill," finally led to his ouster from the Presbyterian Church. Most of the members of his congregation left when he was ousted, and they set up the Community Church of Cincinnati with Maurice McCrackin as their pastor.

On June 16th the IRS struck again.

On June 16th the IRS struck again. They sent four squad cars to the home of Juanita Nelson in Philadelphia. Several deputies and policemen asked Mrs. Nelson to accompany them to a hearing before a United States Commissioner. Juanita refused (she had refused a summons in March and had written to the tax men that she would not cooperate with them). Two deputies and two policemen carried Juanita, who was in her bathrobe, into one of the waiting cars, and took her to the courthouse.

The commissioner told Juanita that she was guilty of contempt and that he could imprison her for a year and impose a fine up to a thousand dollars. He gave Juanita until June 19th to answer questions and to produce records. Juanita did not go to that hearing. On August 8th, the United States attorney in Philadelphia announced that charges against Juanita Nelson had been dropped.

During the spring and summer of 1959, I received several notices to appear before the IRS. I was sent a preliminary report that stated that I owed $2,373.18 in back taxes and penalties for the years 1956 and 1957.

I never knew exactly what my status was as far as taxes were concerned. The government figures were always confusing, but this report indicated how much in a dream world they were.

Let us examine the figures for 1957. That year the report said I made $7,204.05. My family will be glad to know that. I earned $2,760.25 from four companies. The remaining $4,443.80, which the government said I earned while self-employed, was arrived at as follows:

number of weeks in year	52
number of work hour in a week	40
work hours in a year	2080
hours worked as an employee	773
hours self-employed	1307
union scale per hour	3.40
self-employed income	4443.80
wages	2760.25
self-employment income	4443.80
total income	7204.05

$376.20 was withheld by the four companies that employed me. Tax on $7,204.05 comes to $1,279.64 leaving a balance of $903.44, which was charged against me as "delinquent taxes." The IRS added s 25 percent delinquency penalty of $225.86 and a 5 percent negligence penalty of $45.17 to that figure.

Painting is a seasonal trade, and it is an exceptional painter who is able to work 40 hours a week for 52 weeks of the year. I think I deserve a medal for being something of a magician as a painter, because I was 67 years old, my eyes were failing me making it possible for me to work outside only during the warm months, and I had had an operation on my arm partially incapacitating me making it impossible for me to erect scaffolds, etc., by myself.

When I received a notice on November 4th to appear, I wrote a letter stating that I would not be present and that I believed that by appearing I would be offering more cooperation than I cared to give. I told them that I would not respond again to a summons in this matter of trying to collect money from me for war.

I began another period of waiting. I was not working now, so I had plenty of time to wait. I did not know if or when the government would take me on another "vacation" at its expense.

Commissioner Dana Latham informed me on December 11th, by registered letter, "that the determination of income tax liability for the taxable years December 31, 1956, and December 31, 1957, discloses deficiencies in tax aggregating $2,201.73, and penalties aggregating $597.65, as shown in the statement attached."

Chapter Twenty-One

A Woman of Strength

On January 26, 1960, several United States marshals went to the Bethlehem Community Center in Chicago to arrest Eroseanna Robinson — a social worker, track star, and tax refuser. Eroseanna, better known as Sis or Rose, declined to go with the marshals because she felt, like Maurice McCrackin and Juanita Nelson, that any cooperation with the arrest would be cooperation with the government's attempt to get her to pay taxes for war.

She was carried before a judge in the Federal District Court in Chicago. When she refused to stand, the marshals dumped her on the floor. The judge continued the case to the next day.

Sis stopped eating the moment she was arrested, and friends set up an around-the-clock vigil in front of the court building.

When she was carried back into the court the next day, Judge Edwin Robson asked her if she was properly represented by legal counsel. Sis indicated that she did not want a lawyer. The judge urged her to cooperate with the court in turning over her financial records, but she refused. When he permitted her to speak to him as a woman to a man, she said: "I have not filed income taxes because I know that a large part of the tax will be used for militarization. Much of the money is spent for atom and hydrogen bombs. These bombs have a deadly fall-out that causes human destruction, as it has been proved. If I pay income tax, I am participating in that course. We have a duty to contribute constructively to life, and not destructively."

The judge called her attitude one of "contumacious contempt" and ridiculed the around-the-clock vigil going on outside. He had her returned to a jail cell, handcuffed and in a wheelchair, until such time as she would signify a willingness to file a return and produce records of her earnings.

While the vigil continued outside the building, a weekly picketing was set up in New York City. Sis continued her fast and was finally transferred to a hospital where she was force fed through tubes in her nose beginning February 15th.

On February 18th, Judge Robson had Sis Robinson brought before him again. When she still refused to yield her convictions, the judge sentenced her to a year and a day in the Alderson (West Virginia) federal prison.

Karl Meyer, head of a Catholic Worker House of Hospitality in Chicago for down-and-out men, who was instrumental in setting up the around-the-clock vigil, said: "We have been accomplices to crime because we whispered at the moment when we should have shouted. It is time for us to throw up to the state the challenge of Thoreau and Tolstoy — to keep all just men in jail or to give up war and slavery."

He walked into the federal building and began to distribute leaflets on Sis's imprisonment and the immorality of paying for war. He was arrested and sentenced to three days in jail. When he was released, he returned to the federal building and distributed leaflets again. This time he was charged with loitering and sentenced to fifteen days. After Karl returned a third time, the judge ordered a mental examination. Karl was held for 30-days psychiatric examination and then sentenced to 20 days in jail.

Terry Sullivan, who worked with Karl in the House of Hospitality, then went into the federal building and passed out the same leaflets. He also received 30 days in jail for doing so.

Peacemakers decided to support Sis with a picketing at the Internal Revenue Service in Washington. I started it off, with Wally Nelson, another tax-refuser (Juanita is his wife), on March 13th. We picketed every weekday during the office hours of the IRS. We were determined to go through April 15th, income tax deadline day, and the day that tax-refusers from different sections of the country would arrive in Washington for a tax strike against war.

As Wally and I were preparing our signs on the morning of the 13th, a lieutenant from the Washington, D.C., police department came up and asked us when we were going to burn our tax forms. We were startled by this question, because it was only an idea that had been tossed out at a Peacemaker conference and had not been decided upon or publicized. Wally smiled and said, "Not today." The lieutenant persisted and informed us that it was illegal to burn anything on public property.

When he told us that he and the two other policemen were there to protect us, I told him that we didn't need any protecting. The lieutenant answered that they were there to protect everybody.

Wally, who had spent several years in jail after walking out of a civilian public service camp in World War II, remarked later that he was glad that they were there to "protect" us outside on the street, because his memories of being "protected" inside in jail were not so pleasant. The lieutenant departed, leaving the others to protect us. They disappeared after a few days.

We donned our signs, which read: "No Tax for War," "We Support Rose Robinson," "War is Immoral, It's Suicide," "Join the Tax Strike Against War," and began to picket.

On the whole, the response to our demonstration was favorable. As was usual, a few people called us Communists, but several said that our picket line was the most popular in Washington because it was against taxes. Often cars would pull up to us and ask who this Rose Robinson was. Once I felt a hand in my side pocket. I thought it might be a pickpocket but it turned out to be a lady who had just placed a chocolate bar there.

Charles Jackson, Al Uhrie, Miriam Cornelius, and Juanita Nelson — all tax refusers — joined the line at different times before April 15th. Dave Finke of Oberlin College, J. Worrell and George Barrus of Washington also picketed with us in support of Sis Robinson.

During our month in front of the IRS, we passed out many thousands of leaflets. Employees in the Justice Department and the Internal Revenue Service saw us every day. Al Uhrie, Marj Swann, Charles Jackson, Wally Nelson and others had all paid visits on James Bennett, director of the Bureau of Prisons, and on officials in the Justice Department expressing their concern and identification with Sis. This, along with the picketing in Chicago and New York, and of course Sis's continuing non-cooperation and fasting in prison, was making some impression upon the government.

We hoped that the government officials and workers and the passersby were considering the questions which we posed in our leaflets: "Shall the scientists and the military, in the Pentagon and the Kremlin, be given a blank check with which to squander our lives, our honor, and the future of our children — perhaps to destroy the human race? Must the citizen resign his conscience to the government? What is a person's duty when his entire being tells him that the authorities are wrong?"

During several of the weekends off from picketing the IRS, I participated in vigils at the biological warfare center at Fort Detrick, Maryland, and the Army Chemical Center at Edgewood, Maryland.

The vigil at the gates of Fort Detrick, initiated by Lawrence Scott, protested the development of anthrax, cholera, plague, and other disease germs for the destruction of disabling of populations in the event of war. People from all over the country came to stand in front of the gates to protest the psychotic behavior of those who were preparing for such warfare. Science had spent billions of dollars to rid this world of such disease germs, and now some scientists were making it possible to let loose such suffering once again upon this earth.

Dr. LeRoy D. Fothergill, a special adviser to the Fort Detrick monstrosity, said when questioned about the vigil: "We pay no attention to them, and neither does the town." I am glad that I went to Fort Detrick, and I am a little horrified at this man's reaction and at the apathy of the citizens of this country to what is going on there. I am also glad that I am refusing to pay taxes which make possible the unleashing of disease germs upon innocent men, women, and children.

The vigil at the Army Chemical Center in Edgewood, sponsored by CNVA, protested the development of paralyzing nerve gases, poison gases, and other chemicals for the deranging of human beings, While it is not easy to know where our tax money goes these days, with hidden figures to provide for Central Intelligence Agency projects such as the overthrow of the legally-elected Guatemalan government, it was revealed that the budget for chemical and bacteriological warfare in 1960 was $7,000,000 with forecasts that it would go up to $200,000,000 within seven or eight years.

On Friday, April 15th, about thirty tax refusers arrived in Washington for the Tax Strike Against War. Similar picketing went on that day in other sections of the country, including Chicago, Salt Lake City, New York, and Tujunga, California.

Our leaflets and signs proclaimed that a free man's alternative to paying taxes was to refuse to pay them, that the power to tax today was the power to destroy, and that we were reclaiming the right to decide that the money we earned shall not be used for war and other purposes we believed to be evil.

While we walked up and down with our signs in front of the Internal Revenue Service, an FBI agent approached Ernest Bromley (now the editor of *The Peacemaker*, the official organ of the Peacemaker movement) and asked the name of the leader of the demonstration.

"We have no leader," Ernie replied.

"What?" the agent said unbelievingly and somewhat annoyed at this apparent insubordination, "You've got to have a leader." Ernie explained that we were individuals who had come from different states of the country and that we were all responsible for our own actions. In that sense, we were all leaders.

"What is your name and address?" the agent asked.

"I don't think I want to tell you that. We've come here to demonstrate peaceably, which is within our rights, and I don't intend to be intimidated by you."

The agent went down the line to ask each picketer his name and address. Each one refused to tell him. When he got to me, I did not know what the others had done, I told him my name, my address, my age, my birthplace, about my arrests, the fact I had been a Communist, that I was expelled from the Communist Party, etc.

Another agent continued this childish game of intimidation by photographing each of us individually. This is a tactic they often use with picket lines apparently in the hope of discouraging people from participating in them. Perry Ostroff, one of the demonstrators, decided that he wanted a picture of the government photographer. When he snapped it, the agent stormed at him, saying that he couldn't do that.

At noon, we went inside the IRS building to request an interview with Commissioner Dana Latham. His secretary told us that he was out of town but that we could probably see the director of public relations. We were greeted cordially by this man, and we spent an hour explaining the philosophy behind our refusal. The FBI agent who had talked with us on the street was sitting at the far end of the room with a half dozen or so other men, listening to what we had to say.

After the interview, we decided to march to the White House to picket there for a while. The police had warned us that we would be arrested if we walked through the streets of Washington with our signs. We carried them anyway and were not arrested.

When we arrived at the White House, we found three different groups of pickets. The first group consisted of about a hundred and fifty students from Ivy League colleges who were demonstrating their support for sit-ins at southern lunch counters. The second "group" consisted of one man who said on his sign that he was opposed to celestial annexations, whatever that means, and the third group consisted of fellow pacifists who had walked to the White House from the Army Chemical Center in Edgewood to oppose nerve gas and germ warfare. We joined this group, which was sponsored by CNVA.

According to an Associated Press story that appeared in many papers throughout the country:

> ...the pickets were so thick around the White House Friday there was scarcely room for the tourists.... There wasn't room for another queue, but a new batch of demonstrators arrived. This group says it opposes paying taxes for war. They had carried signs Friday morning in front of the Internal Revenue Service, although IRS commissioner Dana Latham was out of town.
>
> Then they straggled up to the White House to bring their message to President Eisenhower, who isn't home either. He is on a golfing vacation in Augusta, Ga.
>
> The first of this group to arrive was Max Sandin of Cleveland, Ohio, and a little girl, perhaps 11 years old, who didn't give her name.

Sandin studied the congestion, then decided to join the group opposing nerve gas and germ warfare, the Committee for Non-Violent Action, New York.

The child demurred. "I feel much more strongly about segregation," she said. Sandin, a spry and tanned little man of 70, smiled and said: "You are young. You go picket wherever you want."

After the demonstration, Ralph Templin, Hank Dyer, Ernie Bromley, Jolee Fritz, Robert Auerbach, Ray Olds, Robert Swann, Marjorie Swann, and Juanita Nelson traveled to Alderson, West Virginia, where they picketed the prison. Ernie Bromley tried to see Sis Robinson, and even put a call into James Bennett in Washington, but to no avail. Sis, in effect, was being held incommunicado, because she would not cooperate with her arrest by walking anywhere in the prison, even to the visiting room and the prison officials refused to let anyone go to her cell, and she would not sign permission for the officials to read her mail, so all mail was sent back to the senders. In the past, the prison bureau has made exceptions to the visiting and mail regulations, but they were out to break Sis Robinson, and they weren't going to make any exceptions in her case.

On May 14th, ten Peacemakers began a fast of indefinite length outside the Alderson prison gates in support of Eroseanna Robinson. They slept outside the gates in sleeping bags and in their cars, placed an ad in the local paper, and made contact with the local townspeople.

Ernest Bromley, Bill Henry, Charles Jackson, Dave Dellinger, Al Uhrie, Trudi Marks, Marjorie Swann, Wallace Nelson, Arthur Harvey, and Clay Marks learned on May 20th that Sis was to be released that very day. They prepared a huge sign saying "Bravo, Rose." The prison officials rushed Sis out of the gates, past the vigilers, down about a mile to the railroad station, just in time to place her on a train for her parent's home in Cleveland. The demonstrators thought in advance that the government would try to prevent her from seeing her friends, so they jumped into two vehicles and also raced to the station. Sis did not get on the train as she was told to, but walked over to her friends. Later, she broke her 93-day fast, and they their 7-day fast at the home of a couple in Alderson that had befriended the group.

Eroseanna Robinson's determination and noncooperation had been too much for the government. This was a woman who had refused to participate in a government-sponsored track team that was to tour Europe because she felt that the government was exploiting the fact that she was a Negro to cover up the actual conditions that Negroes have to live under in this country. This was a woman who probably would have been chosen for the Olympic team if she had not held to her convictions in paying for war and winding up in prison. The government had not succeeded in breaking her will, so they released her after only a fourth of a prison sentence had been forced upon her.

Eroseanna Robinson is greeted by supporters on her release from Alderson Prison, April 1960. Peacemakers photo.

CHAPTER TWENTY-TWO

Trespassing

On August 6, 1960, I bought a window shade, cut a hole in the middle, and made myself a sandwich sign. On one side, I wrote "No More Hiroshimas," and on the other, "Refuse to Pay Income Tax for War." Because I had not been able to interest anyone else in Cleveland in picketing with me in memory of the one hundred thousand men, women, and children killed in Hiroshima 15 years ago, even though nuclear weapons are many more times as powerful as that bomb that fell on Hiroshima, I went down to the federal building and picketed by myself. I was happy to learn later that two thousand people demonstrated in New York on that day.

In the middle of August, I traveled to New London, Connecticut to participate in the Peacemaker Training Program in Nonviolence, which was being held that year in conjunction with the Committee for Nonviolent Action's Polaris Action project against the construction of missile-bearing submarines.

At the training program, an annual affair which brings together new people with individuals active in the nonviolence movement, we participated in discussions with Rev. Fred Shuttlesworth who was having his troubles with Bull Connor in Birmingham, and whose children had been dragged off a bus and threatened by a mob that month in Gadsden, Alabama; Rev. Maurice McCrackin, Eroseanna Robinson, Juanita Nelson, and Karl Meyer, who had been having their troubles with tax officials; Anne Braden, whose husband was in jail for refusing to testify before the Senate Internal Security Committee, and whose home had been bombed by segregationists in Louisville, Kentucky; and others.

Between meetings, we participated in the activities of the Polaris Action campaign. From its headquarters in New London, opened earlier in the summer, several peace walks, leafletings, and picketings were planned and carried out.

The picketings took place either at the navy submarine base or the Electric Boat Yards, about a mile apart, across the river Thames from New London in Groton.

Polaris submarines had become the symbol of this country's massive retaliation capacity. Each submarine was able to launch missiles, within fifteen minutes, that contained several times the explosive power of all the bombs dropped by American planes in World War II. The submarines were being constructed by the Electric Boat Company, a division of General Dynamics Corporation, the largest arms manufacturer in the United States.

Polaris Action's office became the scene of many hot and many reasoned discussions with sailors, some of whom served on Polaris submarines, and with townsfolk. The office had been attacked several times by teenagers.

On August 26th, Polaris Action engaged in its first civil disobedience action. After notifying officials, Bradford Lyttle, the project's coordinator, Margaret Windus (Haworth), Bill Henry, and Julius Jacobs crossed the Thames in a rowboat and climbed aboard the dock at the Electric Boat Yards. They had expected to be arrested, but instead the guards carried them to the gates where quite a few of us were vigiling and dumped them. The following day, the same group with the addition of Richard Zink returned to the dock by boat, climbed onto it, and were carried out again.

I decided to join a third civil disobedience attempt on August 29th. That day twelve of us rowed across the river in several boats, boarded the dock, and went limp when told that we were trespassing. We were carried into waiting cars as the two other groups had been, driven to the gates, and dumped outside.

Each time we had committed civil disobedience, the workers stopped and watched what was going on. At lunch break, hundreds of workers poured out of the boat yards to restaurants across the street. We were able to talk with many of them. While some were hostile, others were not. The question that some asked, "What can I do if I quit my job?" was a difficult one to answer. Many of them were used to the high wages of a war industry, and to give up the luxuries that these wages could buy was a step that many of them could not see themselves taking, even though they admitted that another war would be horrible.

On August 31st, the Polaris submarine, *George Washington*, had just returned to the dock after firing two missiles on target from underwater. Nine more Polaris Actionists announced that they were going to board the submarine. They were escorted away when they reached the dock. The submarine had been raised above the water in the dry dock.

Polaris Action changed its tactics and decided to invade the Navy's submarine base. I decided to join the three young men who were going to enter the base. All previous civil disobedience demonstrations had been at the boat yard, which was under civilian control, but this one would be at a military base, and we thought that we would be arrested.

In explaining his reasoning for committing civil disobedience, Victor Richman said in his preliminary statement:

> An awesome specter threatens me now, invading the seclusion of the most precious parts of my existence, carelessly flaunting its meaning and visions, identifying itself, terribly, with my being. I try, perhaps, to write a poem, to discuss the specter with others, to think seriously about it, and yet it remains, ever conscious of my movement, always ready to inhibit and restrict. It will be at times a dark, inky mist, blocking my path, surrounding me finally, so that I might only flounder helplessly, grope stupidly somewhere for assistance. It appears also as a hard steel chain penetrating insidiously far below my skin, to hold the molecules of my body, to make them frigid, and, thus, cold and uneventful. And I have discovered, eventually, that I am not free.
>
> Can I ever hope to create once more a poem if my body is not free?
>
> Is it possible that I am so strange, so precisely mechanical a being that I might distinguish between my mind and my body?

I have been told that I must not refrain from learning to kill. I have also been told that I must prepare myself in every way for my annihilation. And I have been told that I cannot be present at the places where these conditions are set down. I have not the right to obey these conditions; I have not the right to forbid myself to sing. It will be my body, then that shall sing its song.

You have sung a song of yourself, Walt

And I am singing one of myself;

So, we sing of each other.

And of the world we can see only through ourselves,

And, also, which is contained entirely in ourselves.

After holding a silent meeting at Polaris Action headquarters, 42 persons from Polaris Action and the Peacemaker Continuation Committee began a five-mile walk to the submarine base in Groton.

At the base we joined two others who had been part of an all-night vigil. Victor [Richman], Peter [Friedlander], Torvald [Faegre], and I went forward. There were marines everywhere. We were stopped and questioned about our intentions. The sentries informed us that we were trespassing, but we continued to walk into the base. The boys were grabbed by the marines. I walked a few feet more, before a marine took me by the arm and pushed me toward the base office.

We were brought before the Commanding Officer who asked us our reasons for entering. Peter told him that we were protesting the arms race. Everyone in the room seemed nervous except for the Commanding Officer. He told us that we were trespassing and that we would be led out of the base.

"What are your names?" We told him.

He gave us a sheet of paper, which said that we would be arrested if we entered the base again and could be fined up to $500 or imprisoned for more than six months, or both.

I refused my copy and instead offered the Commanding Officer a copy of the *Polaris Action Bulletin*, which contained our reasons for entering the base. Then I sat down on a sofa next to the officer and the nurse. They arose immediately.

"You are not allowed to sit down," the Commanding Officer said, losing his composure.

I told him that I was tired from the five-mile walk.

Peter, Torvald, and Victor sat down next to me.

"We have no seats for you," he commanded impatiently.

We made it clear that we were not going to cooperate with our removal from the base. The Commanding Officer ordered the guards to get a stretcher and to carry me out to a truck. He told them to be careful.

As I was being placed in the truck, someone snapped my photograph for the government's voluminous files. My companions were dragged out of the office and thrown into the truck on top of each other. We could not see where we were being taken, but the ride seemed much longer than the distance from the gate to the office. The trees above seemed to nod their approval of what we had done. After quite a while we were deposited at another gate miles from nowhere. Eventually, a Polaris Action car arrived.

My three companions decided to enter the base a second time. I was tired, and I had said earlier that I would enter only once. I felt I had done my duty, and my conscience was clear. They were ejected again. Apparently, the navy had learned a lesson in nonviolence from us.

In subsequent months, many of the Polaris Actionists were arrested and spent several months up to a year in jail for their efforts against the war effort. Polaris Action continues as a community project to this day, however, under the direction of Marjorie and Robert Swann. Marj, who has four children, spent six months in the Alderson Federal prison earlier that year for attempting to climb the fence at an Intercontinental Ballistic Missile Base near Omaha, Nebraska, in the summer of 1959 (a project under CNVA's sponsorship). Bob subsequently spent six months in jail for his activities at Polaris Action.

CHAPTER TWENTY-THREE

The Leaderless Vanguard

Max Sandin circa early 1960s. Photo courtesy of Deborah Tenenbaum.

The federal government continued in its efforts to force pacifists to pay for war preparation when it sent its agents to Mount Vernon, Iowa, to arrest Walter Gormly, a consultant engineer. It met with the same stubborn determination and resistance that the previously arrested tax refusers had presented. Gormly had to be carried to the courthouse. He refused to move voluntarily from one place to another. He talked whenever he thought it was necessary and appropriate to do so, disregarding the formalities of the court. When asked to produce his financial records, he told the judge that he would not, and neither would he pay the $8,200 the Internal Revenue Service said he owed. Although Gormly said he would not appear, Judge Henry Graven set November 28th as the date for the next hearing and released him.

The tax refuser told the judge in a letter that the $8,200 figure the IRS said he owed was fantasy and had no relationship to his income for the years in question. He also argued that the tax collecting agency had no right to assess penalties for "underestimation of tax" or for failure to file a declaration of estimated tax on time. "The Internal Revenue Service does not come into court with clean hands," he said. "Its hands are dirtied with its own law violations.... Its hands have on them the blood of those who have died and will die of cancer and other diseases caused by radioactive fallout. Its hands are polluted with the blood of children who have been or will be born defective...."

On December 20th Walter Gormly was carried back into the courtroom and sentenced to a jail term of seven days for contempt of court in failing to produce records and other information leading to a collection. The judge told Walter that he would be released any time before his sentence was up if he agreed to produce his records.

After spending a few days, involuntarily, at the Linn County Jail, Gormly who was on a hunger strike, was transferred to a hospital in Cedar Rapids to undergo intravenous feeding. Once again, the government found its efforts in vain. He was released on December 27th.

Sometime in the middle of March, Eroseanna Robinson equaled the record for the high jump in the National AAU women's championships in Cleveland. On March 15th, Jack Clowser of the *Cleveland Press* wrote:

When I asked her where she'd been at last year's meet, she calmly replied, "In prison."

"Yes, that's why I wasn't competing last year," she said. "I'm a conscientious objector to war. For me, that means I also object to paying income taxes which go to buy the weapons people are killed with. So, they sentenced me to federal penitentiary for a year and a day."

I had met Rose before. Her sister, Mrs. Bernice Holland of Cleveland, was a member of the 1948 U.S. Olympic team that went to London. But this was the first time I knew of Rose's deep convictions about human slaughter. She's unmarried, and does settlement house work in Philadelphia — helping those who have the least in life. That's dedication.

"Rose," I said, "I wish I had your guts. I hate war, too. But I wouldn't have the moral courage to go to prison for my feelings about it."

All right, realists, I know if none of us paid federal taxes, the many worthwhile pursuits of government would wither, too. But imagine, what would happen if, in every country, people stopped paying land and property taxes against the armaments race.

Pacifists are looked upon as nuts. Still, you'll have to admit they're following the teachings of Christianity.

I traveled to Washington once again to take up my picketing before the IRS building some weeks before another Tax Strike Against War. I stayed at Fellowship House, a settlement house in a poor section of Washington, as I had the previous year. Joan Ohrenstein, the director, greeted me warmly. She treated me like a brother and understood what I was doing. For her kindnesses and those of Abby Hadley, a teacher at Fellowship House, I have grown to love them like my daughters. Several times, the three of us went out on picket lines at Woolworth's and other stores in support of equal rights for Negroes.

On April 1st, I took time out from my picketing of the IRS to stand in front of the Pentagon with about a hundred other persons in a vigil protesting nuclear armaments. We held signs such as "The World Is Now too Small for Anything but Brotherhood." We called upon the United States government to take the initiative in ending nuclear tests. We asked for the abolition of chemical and biological weapons and for the conversion of Fort Detrick into a world health center.

After the vigil, which was called "Witness for Peace," we walked across the Potomac to Judiciary Square in Washington where James Baldwin spoke to about four hundred people linking the peace and integration movements. The demonstration, which was sponsored by 14 groups favoring disarmament, was picketed by George Rockwell's Nazis.

Back on the line in front of the IRS, I was joined at times by Wally Nelson and Ross Anderson, and on April 15th, five other tax refusers joined us. After presenting our statements of refusal to a representative of the IRS, we walked to the White House where the police approached us immediately, asking for our leaders and the name and addresses of the participants. We told the police, as we had the FBI agent the year before, that we had no leader. Their reaction was the same — one of disbelief. "There has to be a leader!"

A few minutes later, another squad car arrived and five policemen got out. They also could not believe us when we told them we had no leader. We kept on picketing. After discussing this strange situation among themselves, they picked out Arthur Harvey and asked him for his name and address, that of all the other demonstrators, and the place where we were staying. Arthur told them his name but refused to give then any more information. Next, they went to Ernie Bromley, who told them that he didn't care to register himself with the police. The officer questioning Ernie tried to impress upon him that it was only for our protection that they were asking these questions, but Ernie was not impressed.

I returned to Cleveland just in time to meet the San Francisco to Moscow Peace walkers who were to spend three days there from April 21st to April 23rd. The forty walkers, some of whom had come all the way across the continent from San Francisco, picketed several military installations, factories making war materials, the draft board and the Internal Revenue Service while they were in Cleveland. I joined them in several of these pickets and walked with them for a while.

Karl Meyer and another walker stayed at my house one night, and on Sunday I drove Karl to a Catholic Church for mass. Of course, I didn't go in, but I came back after the service for him. My wife and I visited our son in Wooster, and upon our return, we met the walkers along the highway. We made three trips transporting tired walkers to the place they were to stay that night.

That summer, I planned to picket in the Public Square on Hiroshima Day and to travel to Voluntown, Connecticut, to participate in another Peacemaker training program in nonviolence. Little did I know that I was to be the next victim in the government's campaign to get everyone to conform to preparing for war.

CHAPTER TWENTY-FOUR

The IRS and My Livelihood

Instead of receiving my monthly Social Security check of $116 on the third day of August, I received the following letter from the Department of Health, Education, and Welfare, Social Security Administration, Bureau of Old-Age and Survivors Insurance, Payment Center:

August 1, 1961

Dear Mr. Sandin:

In compliance with a Notice of Levy issued by the Internal Revenue Service of the Treasury Department under Section 6331, Internal Revenue Code of 1954, your social security benefit for July 1961 has been surrendered to the Internal Revenue Service.

Sincerely yours,
Joseph J. Tighe
Chief, Payment Center

Several times before the IRS had threatened to take away my Social Security checks, but still this letter came as a shock. The Internal Revenue was leaving me with only a $31.20 pension check from the Painting Industry Insurance Fund to live on this month. But maybe the tax men would even take that. What would they do in future months? I had received a letter on February 9th stating that I owed an unpaid balance of $1,363.71 for 1956 and $1,702.88 for 1957. Now that the IRS has taken one Social Security check it seemed reasonable to assume that they would continue to do so until they collected all that they said I owed. I decided that if the government was going to starve me, it might as well do it while I was sitting in at the Treasury Building in Washington, so that government officials could see what they were doing to me.

Before going to Washington, I picketed in the Public Square on August 6th in memory of the 100,000 human beings killed in Hiroshima. It was hard to believe that men and women were still dying from that blast which happened sixteen years ago. About a dozen other persons were picketing there from the Cleveland Committee for a Sane Nuclear Policy and from Youth for Progressive Action, but they didn't want me to join them because I wore a sign which said "Refuse to Pay Income Tax for War," as well as "No More Hiroshimas."

I decided to picket by myself instead of covering up my belief in not paying for another Hiroshima. (I joined them for a newspaper photograph, however, with only the latter sign.)

I went to Voluntown, Connecticut, to attend the Peacemaker training program in nonviolence for a few days. After that I stopped by the CNVA office in New York where David Munro, a college professor, said he would like to help by going to the IRS in Washington with me as a representative of CNVA. We spent all of August 29th talking with officials in the IRS and going over the law with them. We were told by IRS officials that I would have to go home to Cleveland to argue my case there.

Robert Crater, Washington correspondent for the *Cleveland Press*, wrote in a dispatch about our interviews:

> Late in the day, IRS spokesmen admitted there was a possible legal loop-hole through which Sandin might wriggle, should he choose to do so.
>
> "The Social Security law says no one can attach the payments to individuals, but our law doesn't except the beneficiaries," explained Lawrence George, spokesman for the tax-collection service. "There's possible conflict in this case that could be taken to court."

Sandin said he wouldn't fight his battle in court....

Max hasn't much to offer in a hunger strike. Besides his advanced age, he's only five feet two inches tall and weighs 132 pounds.

Max says the Social Security checks he had been getting are all that is between him and starvation, so he has decided to starve for all to see, at the Treasury.

According to the *Washington Evening Star* of August 30th,

Said one IRS official here after a conference with Mr. Sandin: "If he thinks the action taken by the service is illegal, he can take the matter to court."

Privately, another official said — when it was pointed out IRS had a public relations problem in a possible starvation case at their doors: "What's that old saw about an irresistible force meeting an immovable object?"

The Internal Revenue knew very well that I didn't have the money to take this case into court, if I wanted to. One of its officials had even questioned the legality of its actions, but apparently it can interpret the laws as it sees fits and then leave it up to the individual affected to challenge its decision.

On the morning of August 30th, I joined members of the Peace Action Center on their line in front of the White House. At 11 o'clock I went to the Treasury building, which was right next to the White House, to request an interview with Secretary of Treasury C. Douglas Dillon. His secretary said that he wasn't in. I then went out into the corridor and sat down outside of Dillon's office. Two Secret Service agents came over to me and asked me my intentions. I told them that my Social Security check had been seized by the government and that if the government planned to starve me it should see me starved. I told them that I was going on a sit in and hunger strike until my check was returned and that I would not leave the building when it closed.

They whisked me upstairs to their office where they questioned me. Soon two city policemen came to take me in a patrol wagon to police headquarters. While I was waiting for something to happen, the policemen in the station were making remarks. One of them said "You son-of-a-bitch, you're a Jew and you wouldn't fight for your country."

From there, several policemen asked me to go with them in their car. I told them that I wanted to make a phone call but they wouldn't let me, so I sat down on the floor. They decided to let me make the call. After that, I was driven to the District of Columbia General Hospital where I was placed in the psychiatric ward.

While I was being held in the psychiatric ward, Joseph J. Ellis, Jr., Special Agent, United States Secret Service, petitioned the U.S. District Court for the District of Columbia to have me detained for observation and examination. He said in his petition:

> At about 11:30 a.m., August 30, 1961 the above subject appeared at the main Treasury Building for the purpose of staging a sit-in and hunger strike. He is a conscientious objector and refused to pay income tax because taxes are used for military purposes. Internal levied against his Social Security checks. Sandin sat in the corridor, with his back to the wall, outside the office of the Secretary of the Treasury. When interviewed by the reporting Agent, he reported that he would refuse to leave the building when closed for the day, and that he intended to starve himself to death, if necessary, in the Treasury Building, until his Social Security checks were restored. He refused to answer questions about himself and became withdrawn as the interview progressed.
>
> In view of his condition and his inability to take care of himself, it was felt necessary to admit him to D.C. General Hospital for mental observation.
>
> Your petitioner is informed, and believes and therefore avers said patient is of unsound mind, incapable of managing his own affairs; and within the purview of the stature in that case made and provided, it is not desirable to permit him to go about unsupervised, and he is a proper subject for commitment to a hospital for treatment.

Judge George L. Hart, Jr., considered the petition on the following day and "ordered, that Max Sandin be detained in District of Columbia General Hospital for thirty days hereafter, unless meanwhile discharged therefrom or transferred to Saint Elisabeth's Hospital, and pending further order of this Court."

Stephen D. Pfeiffer, a young conscientious objector who lives in Washington, D.C., decided to support me by sitting in at the Treasury building on September 1st. His story which appeared in *The Peacemaker* of September 9th is as follows:

After having sat for about 45 minutes (4:45 p.m.) two Secret Service police came up to me and told me that I would have to leave by 5:30 p.m. and if I refused, I would be picked up bodily and put out of the building. At about 5:00 p.m., the same two Secret Service police agents returned and told me I was to leave the building by the 15th Street entrance. If I did not do so, I would be put under arrest. I then asked what charge I would be put under and they said disorderly conduct. That I was disturbing the employees' work, and I told them I was nonviolently and peaceably sitting out of the way of people coming and leaving the building. They told me that employees were being forced to look at my sign, which read "VIGIL and FAST, NO TAXES FOR WAR, WORK FOR PEACE," and that this was considered disorderly conduct. They then took me to their office, asked me some questions and finally turned me over to the Metropolitan police of Washington, D.C. to be booked.

Stephen Pfeifer received a $25 fine, which was suspended.

I remained on my hunger strike for four days and then decided to give it up. Because I had to remain in the hospital for 30 days, and they weren't mistreating me, I decided that my protest in itself was enough, and secondly, I wanted to eat.

During my stay at the hospital, I was interviewed by several doctors. One of them commented at the end of an interview "If they will free you, that would embarrass the Internal Revenue Service, and I don't think they would like that."

On September 11th, I received a sanity hearing. Lawrence Scott of Peace Action Center, Dave Dellinger of *Liberation* magazine, Paul Olynyk, chairman of Cleveland Committee for a Sane Nuclear Policy, Joan Ohrenstein and Abby Hadley of Fellowship House, Miriam Cornelius, an editor, Stephen and Lorraine Pfeiffer, and Oliver Stone, who represented me, appeared at the hearing.

The psychiatrist read from notes that I was born on June 3, 1889, in Russia and that I was naturalized in Cleveland, Ohio. Secret Service Agent Ellis told the hearing that "About 11:30 a.m. August 30 on the third floor of the Treasury Building Mr. Sandin was seated with his back to the wall. I asked him what he was doing and he said he was engaged in a hunger strike until his Social Security checks were returned."

Next the panel asked me if I had anything to say. I told the doctors about the incident in *cheder* when I asked my teacher why God had told Saul to "go and smite Amalek and utterly destroy all that they have; do not spare them, but kill both man and woman, infant and suckling, ox and sheep, camel and ass," and how the teacher smacked me across the face knocking out several of my teeth because I was not to question God's words. I told the doctors how I thought this incident had implanted in me the seeds of conscientious objection to war. I could not pay taxes for war I said, as I had not been able to serve in the army in Russia or this country. When the Treasury Department [sent] my Social Security benefits, which helped to keep me alive, to the Internal Revenue Service, I decided to sit there and was ready to die for peace.

When asked if I would return to the Treasury Department, I told them that I did not know what I was going to do next but that I certainly would continue to work for peace.

Oliver Stone told the hearing "Others have taken similar positions. I want to make it clear that Max Sandin should do as his conscience tells him."

Dave Dellinger told the panel that I could stay at his place if I wanted to. When the panel asked "Will you take care of him?" Dave answered "He can take care of himself."

Lawrence Scott told the panel "I share the same convictions as Max Sandin. He is a man of no violence and is within his right. I have known him for about eight years." One of the doctors asked Larry if he refused to pay taxes for the same reason. "Yes, I do. And this is not tax dodging. I have notified the Treasury Deportment of my position."

When the head psychiatrist commented "He seems to be starving himself for no reason at all," Oliver Stone replied "He should feel no strings attached to any release, but should feel [free] to follow his conscience." Stone was asked if he considered me eccentric. "No. If you consider him eccentric, then I would say most of us here in this room are eccentric."

"Does anyone in this room think Max Sandin should be committed to a mental hospital?" the doctor asked. Silence greeted this question. I was released an hour later.

During this kidnapping ordeal, many of my friends came to my aid by writing letters of support. Here are a few of them:

I am writing as an acquaintance of Mr. Max Sandin as well as a social worker with many years of experience in working directly with the mentally ill. I feel I am qualified to testify to the mental status of Mr. Sandin, concerning which a hearing has been scheduled.... At no time have I observed that Mr. Sandin suffered from any symptoms associated with psychosis. His judgment, memory, and intelligence appeared unimpaired.

I am aware that Mr. Sandin's political opinions are unorthodox and that he has chosen to express his views through radical actions. Our nation, however, has always nurtured radicals and some of them, such as Thoreau and Garrison, are today honored in our history.

The perversion of mental health concepts to punish the unorthodox rather than cure the sick would be a far greater danger to our country than can be embodied in this gentle little man. I sincerely hope he will be judged according to the honest and objective standards that psychiatry has struggled so hard to achieve.

Mrs. Netta Berman

I have known Mr. Max Sandin ever since I was called to this congregation three years ago, and I have carefully studied the history of his career of personal testimony against war and violence. I can vouch for the fact that he is a sincerely dedicated individual who means evil to no one, but he is determined to live his life according to principles of conscientious objection for which he is willing to make any sacrifice....

Rabbi Arthur J. Lelyvold,
Fairmount Temple, Cleveland

I have known Max Sandin for two years and his devotion to the cause of world peace has been single-minded and sacrificial. Would that the courage and determination of this frail old man permeated the beings of all the workers for peace! It is hard for the smug and self-satisfied to understand the selflessness of Max Sandin so they ridicule him and heap upon him the crowning indignity subjection to mental observation. I would remind his tormentors to remember that another good man was misunderstood by the quoters of law and scripture two thousand years ago, and deemed mad. I urge the modern-day legalists to set this kind, good, old servant of man at liberty to continue the labor he has been called for.

Dr. Paul Olynyk, Chairman,
The Cleveland Committee for a Sane Nuclear Policy

Any individual in the United States has traditionally been free to appeal to the public conscience, to employers, or to government authorities by peaceful picketing and other demonstrations of a similar nature. If this is still so, why was Max Sandin, on the first day of a nonviolent demonstration at a government agency, seized by officers and confined in D.C. General Hospital to await a sanity hearing?

Mr. Sandin is known to me as an out-spoken, tough-minded, well oriented person. I first met him at a pacifist conference in January 1960. Since then, I have kept in touch with him, and on one occasion he was a dinner guest at my home.

During the time that I have been acquainted with him — and throughout his entire life, I am informed — Mr. Sandin has maintained a principled opposition to war, violence, killing, and the reliance on military force as a means of keeping peace in the world. If these views are a proof of unsound mind, many Quakers, ministers, pacifists — all these, indeed, who take seriously the Commandment "Thou shalt not kill" — are candidates for mental hospitals.

Mr. Sandin's recent demonstration at the U.S. Treasury Department building was intended to arouse the public conscience to a new infringement of civil liberties. This was the garnishment of his small monthly Social Security benefits in toto, in reprisal for his continued refusal to pay past-due war taxes.

I am told that the deposition of the officer who ordered Mr. Sandin locked up stated: "In view of his inability to take care of himself, it was felt best to admit him to the D.C. General Hospital for mental observation." But if Mr. Sandin was not able to take care of himself, it was because the government had stopped his Social Security benefits; like others who received monthly old-age benefits under the Old Age and Survivors Insurance program, Mr. Sandin fully earned the right to them. He followed a skilled trade and paid the Social Security tax (to which of course, he had no objection) until retirement.

As to the nature of Mr. Sandin's demonstration at the Treasury Department, there is well established precedent for use of the "sit in" by pacifists when other peaceful means of appeal have been exhausted. For example:

After World War II, a young minister sat day and night on the steps of the Department of Justice building, appealing for the release of conscientious objectors still in prison. After six months, the last C.O. was released, and the 'steps of Justice' were vacated.

Two or three years ago, a group of pacifists sat day and night in the lobby of the Atomic Energy Commission headquarters at Gaithersburg, Md., seeking an interview with Commissioner Strauss in regard to certain policies of the Commission. After two weeks of maintaining a vigil and fast, they obtained an interview with the Commissioner.

A group of fasting sympathizers camped outside the gate to the Federal Prison for Women in Alderson, W. Va., while Eroseanna Robinson was imprisoned there for refusal to pay war taxes. After a number of days (about a week, I think), Miss Robinson, who had been on hunger strike throughout her imprisonment, was unconditionally released.

In no case was any doubt cast on the sanity of the demonstrators.

Since Mr. Sandin's life-long views, his current financial embarrassment due to government action, and the nature of his protest all have logical explanations, the question arises whether the agencies or persons responsible for locking him up in the D.C. General Hospital psychiatric....[10]

---

[10] *Editors' note: The Uhrie-edited and typed manuscript ended in the middle of that sentence. See the Afterword for further explanation.*

These three men, refusing to pay income tax, show papers explaining their views. Left to right, the Rev. Ernest Bromley, Ross Anderson and Max Sandin.—Star Staff Photo.

3 Pacifists Picket Tax Office, Refuse to Pay for Arms Race

Three men carrying picket signs and posters stationed themselves this morning at the corner of Constitution avenue and Tenth street N.W. in the chill shadow of the Internal Revenue Service Building.

A brisk wind cut into their lined faces and tugged at the frayed sleeves of their overcoats. The busy passersby seemed as indifferent as the wind twirling scraps of paper in its eddies.

After half an hour of peaceful picketing, the three men walked into the building to the third floor office of Mortimer M. Caplin, Commissioner of Internal Revenue.

Ask to See Caplin

In a reception room they introduced themselves to a secretary and said they would like to see Mr. Caplin.

"Mr. Caplin is very busy," the girl replied. "Would you tell me why you wish to see him?"

Their leader, Ernest R. Bromley, a printer and Methodist minister from Cincinnati, Ohio, said the men wanted to explain why they did not intend to pay their income taxes today.

"We are tax refusers," he said. "We don't believe in paying taxes when most of the millions the Government will collect this year will go for war. We are pacifists."

Accompanying Mr. Bromley, who is 50, were Max Sandin,

72, a retired housepainter, of Cleveland, and a tall, gaunt, bearded man named Ross Anderson, 61, a retired Methodist minister and teacher who lives at 2023 Kalorama road N.W.

Now Owes $4,100

Mr. Sandin said he had refused to pay taxes for the last 20 years and said he owed about $4,100. He gave reporters a statement telling how he had been sent to District General Hospital last August after he staged a sit-in and hunger strike at the Treasury Building.

Mr. Bromley said he didn't know how much he owned in taxes and Mr. Anderson said he kept his income low enough so

that he didn't have to pay taxes.

They were taken to a room where Mitchell Rogovin, special assistant to Mr. Caplin, and Joseph Rosapepe, director of information for the service, listened to their complaints about the use of tax money in the arms race.

"We won't do anything," said Mr. Rosapepe. "They came here to say something, so we'll listen."

Downstairs, a long line of taxpayers waited patiently to get last-minute information and pay their taxes before the deadline tonight.

THE EVENING STAR

Washington, D. C.,

Monday, April 16, 1962

Ernest Bromley, Ross Anderson, and Max Sandin picket the national IRS building on tax day in 1962, The Washington Evening Star, April 16, 1962

The Remainder of Max's Life

Following the successful outcome of his September 11, 1961, sanity hearing, the remainder of Sandin's life continued much as it had before. Through 1966 he would picket the IRS every tax day (middle of April), hold his often solitary Hiroshima Day (August 6) vigils for a nuclear test ban treaty and against nuclear weapons in front of the Federal Building in downtown Cleveland, and attend every one of the Peacemaker's summer gatherings (Orientation Program in Nonviolence), which began in 1948.

He would, of course, continue to refuse to voluntarily pay any federal income taxes to the IRS, including a well-publicized 1962 protest with Peacemakers Ernest Bromley and Ross Anderson on tax day in front of the national headquarters of the IRS in Washington, DC. In an April 17, 1962 article headlined "Clevelander Is Among 'Tax Refusers'," the Cleveland *Plain Dealer* noted "Max Sandin, 72, of Cleveland, a retired house painter, said he had refused to pay taxes for 20 years and figured he owed about $4,100."

On August 24, 1962, Sandin was among the 40 people opposed to the death penalty who picketed the Cook County Jail all day into the night trying to stay the execution of cop killer James Duke, who became the last person to be executed by the state of Illinois until 1990 following the reinstatement of the death penalty.

Still plagued by the periodic IRS seizures of his Social Security and retirement checks, Sandin wrote a long letter to President John F. Kennedy on September 25, 1962, saying, in part:

> I DO NOT WANT TO DIE FROM STARVATION. Eichmann, [James] Duke, Max Sandin: These three human beings were sentenced to pay with their lives for the crimes they committed against their fellow human beings. . . . Here are two men who were sentenced to be

killed because they killed, and I was sentenced [to be killed] because I refuse to kill. . . .I am 73 years old and I want to live more and more. I want back my Social Security and my Painters' Union checks for which I have been paid since 1937. I hope that your conscience will be your guide, because I am not asking for mercy or pardon. Please: Do not commit murder. Max Sandin, Washington 10, DC.

In the summer of 1963, Sandin took a bus from the Harlem office of the Congress of Racial Equality in New York City down to Washington, DC, to participate in the August 28 March on Washington for Jobs and Freedom. As it would happen, sitting next to him was a teenage Randy Kehler (see the Foreword to this book for Randy's account).

Beginning at least since 1964, he protested the U.S. war in Vietnam, including signing newspaper ads and joining street protests.

By age 78, it appears his days of street protesting were over, though Max continued to refuse payments to the IRS for the rest of his life. He and his wife Sarah lived with their daughter Irene, her husband Perry Tenenbaum, and granddaughter Debby in Cleveland before he moved into a rest home not long before his death at age 82 on September 14, 1971.

Ruth Benn and Ed Hedemann

The Mystery of a Meandering Manuscript and Its Missing Pages

I n 1920, Max Hayes, a Sandin friend as well as editor and founder of *The Cleveland Citizen*, Cleveland's American Federation of Labor newspaper, urged Sandin write about his imprisonment as a conscientious objector during World War I. Nevertheless, it wasn't until 35 years later (in 1955) while in Miami for four months that he began writing what he initially titled "Political War Objector." That year Bernard Tamerkin, another friend, suggested "I Was Sentenced to Be Shot" would be a catchier title. Sandin estimated he wrote 600 (longhand) pages in English, then a year later translated it into Yiddish. He continued to record stories at least through 1963.

Western Reserve Historical Society (WRHS) in Cleveland, Ohio, is the repository of Sandin's papers, including 369 of the (mostly) handwritten autobiography pages they acquired from his wife Sarah Sandin following Max's 1971 death. Besides being incomplete, regrettably, these pages do not extend beyond 1956.

However, this book is largely based on the typed, restructured, and edited version performed by Al Uhrie,[11] who had access to Max's handwritten pages in the early 1960s. Mysteriously, that edited manuscript abruptly ends mid-sentence at the bottom of page 228, just after the story of Sandin being declared sane following his 1961 Washington, DC court hearing. Ostensibly, the hearing was held because authorities considered his sit-in and fast at the Treasury Department the actions of a madman unable to care for himself.

Tragically, Al was robbed, brutally beaten, and murdered 11 pm on August 17, 1966, by three teenage boys outside of his Lower East Side apartment in

Manhattan. For a while, Barbara, his young wife, and their five-month-old baby Susannah moved 110 miles north of the city to the Catholic Worker farm in Tivoli, NY. Al's papers, which may have included the edited manuscript, were put into storage at the farm but were lost not long after. What survives is a single carbon copy of Uhrie's typed and edited 228-page version plus the partial collection of handwritten pages available at WRHS.

In 1975 Rita Corbin and Dorothy Day of the Catholic Worker donated the 228-page Uhrie-edited manuscript to the Institute for the Study of Nonviolence in Palo Alto, California, founded by Joan Baez and Ira Sandperl. Robert Cooney used the manuscript to aid his research for *The Power of the People*, which was published in 1977. With the Institute closed and learning of Randy Kehler's connection with Max, in 2013 Cooney sent the manuscript to him. Then, in 2022, Randy forwarded it to us, hoping we could find a way to get Max's fascinating and, at times, harrowing adventures published and available to the wider world.

After digitalizing the almost 60-year-old Uhrie-edited version, we compared it to Sandin's extant handwritten pages to help clarify passages and, in the process, restore some of the stories left out of the Uhrie-edited manuscript. On the other hand, we omitted many verbatim articles Max included about himself and other resisters.

Deborah Tenenbaum, Sandin's granddaughter, graciously shared the photos of Max we have used in this book.

Ruth Benn and Ed Hedemann

---

[11] *Al Uhrie, born in 1932, grew up in Ossining, NY, graduated from William & Mary College with a journalism major, was part of the anarchist pacifist commune in Glen Gardner, NJ, in the 1950s, which published* Liberation *magazine. As one of the most active peace workers from the mid-1950s until his death, he was a war tax resister, member of Peacemakers (probably where he met Sandin), War Resisters League, CNVA, Catholic Worker, the Puerto Rican independence movement, Nonviolent Committee for Cuban Independence, among other groups and causes. Uhrie was arrested in 1956 and 1958 for his refusal to take shelter during the civil defense drill protests in NYC; jailed 12 days in Albany, GA, during the 1963 Quebec to Guantanamo Walk for Peace; arrested at the 1965 Assembly of Unrepresented People in Washington, DC. In 1964 he decided to return to college but changed his mind in order to devote full time working for an end to the war in Vietnam. Uhrie was author, with Donna Allen, of the 1965 pamphlet* What's Wrong with the War in Vietnam, *and was a key organizer for the Fifth Avenue Peace Parade Committee as well as other protests at the time of his 1966 death.*

OBITUARY

Max Sandin, Laborer, Resister, Peacemaker

The Peacemaker, October 9, 1971, p. 2

Max Sandin died in a Cleveland, Ohio rest home on September 14, 1971 at the age of 82. For the past few years failing health had kept him from attending Peacemaker meetings or corresponding with people; and many times we heard the question, Where is Max? For 18 years he had come to most of the gatherings.

When participating in discussions, Max often referred to his youth in Russia during the czarist regime. He was fond of stories by Leo Tolstoy, and would sometimes tell one of these in a meeting in order to illustrate a point or lighten the discussion.

In World War I he was a conscientious objector, but soon found himself in army camp. Refusing to train or follow military orders, he was court-martialed and sentenced to be shot. President Wilson later commuted the sentence to 15 years. He continued his noncooperation in the prison at Ft. Leavenworth, Kansas, saying afterward that as far as he could see the army and the prison had little to distinguish them. He was later to complain mildly about the amount of cooperation prisons get from present-day objectors.

In World War II he refused to register when a law was passed to conscript men up to the age of 65. He was arrested but never prosecuted.

In 1943 he commenced to refuse to pay federal income taxes, years before most pacifists thought of such action or were willing to consider it. He did not seem to mind following his best insights even though acting alone.

He took the trouble, as years went by to go where people were imprisoned for war tax nonpayment, and to demonstrate his support of the person and the action. For many years he took a bold picketing position at the entrance of the Internal Revenue headquarters in Washington at 10th St. and Pennsylvania Ave. Each April you could find him there a week ahead of the income tax deadline, with oilcloth sandwich signs and leaflets. People got to know him and called a "Hello Max" in passing. He called on the IRS workers to quit their jobs and the folks coming to pay income taxes to turn homeward. Max had seen much misery and much war, and wanted to spend his life opposing and uprooting it.

In his occupation of house painting his employer wanted to withhold income taxes from his pay. He left the job and found his own houses to paint. There are stories that IRS agents rose early to try to collect some money owed him. They didn't meet with much success, but in 1946 did collect $145 of an assessment against him of $2800.

After retirement he lived on income from Social Security and a pension from the Painters' Union, together making $151 per month. On August 1, 1961, he received from the Social Security office a letter stating that Internal Revenue had commandeered his monthly check for refused taxes. Max protested the seizure by going in person to the headquarters of both Internal Revenue and Social Security in Washington, finally taking up a position at the U. S. Department of the Treasury. Although 72 years old, he commenced a fast, which he said he hoped to continue until the money was restored.

"In World War I," he said, "I was sentenced to be shot for not wanting to kill. Now I am sentenced to starve for not wanting to buy bombs for World War III."

He was arrested for probable insanity and taken to Washington General Hospital's psychiatric ward. Some days later, after a hearing, he was released.

IRS continued to appropriate the Social Security check and also the pension check. They admitted that there was no precedent for taking his Social Security payment but claimed it was legal.

Max, a laborer, not at home in the fields of writing or speaking, did more in his lifetime to help bring in a nonviolent society than almost anyone who comes to mind. Because of his beliefs and activities he did not always find things congenial at home. He would often come to Peacemaker functions and say, "Peacemakers is my family."

He came to almost every Peacemaker gathering that was held. When leaving the 1966 orientation program in nonviolence held in Tivoli, N.Y., in August 1966, he said "This is probably my last time." It was.

E R B [Ernest R. Bromley]

Report on Torture of C.O.s during WW I

From September 5th to October 21st, [C.O.s] were systematically tortured by the officers and guards. A diary of those tortures was read on the floor of the House of Representatives by William E. Mason of Illinois on March 3, 1919. The following quotations are from that diary.[12]

Thursday, September 5, 1918.

Seven conscientious objectors arrived at the military police guardhouse [at Camp Funston] from the guardhouse at Riley.

Saturday, September 7.

We were ordered to fold our arms and stand at attention by the officer of the day, Captain Buckley. Failing to comply with this order, he proceeded to abuse and insult us, referring to those of Jewish birth as "damn kikes," etc. He then had our beds and blankets taken from us and ordered that we be given raw rations — pork and beans — which we were to cook in the latrine, if we wanted to eat. He suggested to the prisoners that they beat us up. We had no supper and slept on the bare floor in our clothes.

Sunday, September 8.

Very little sleep was had because of the extreme chilliness of the night.

No other provisions having been made for the preparation of food; we ate nothing on this day.

We again slept on the bare floor without blankets.

---

[12] *The following quotations are from that diary. It can also be read in full online by searching on "Report of Treatment of Conscientious Objectors at the Camp Funston," which will include a link to Swarthmore College Peace Collection's copy, among others.*

Monday, September 9.

Food conditions remained the same until supper when we were informed that a kitchen for preparing our food would be furnished us if we would do our own cooking. We were able to prepare supper. Upon returning from this meal, we were informed that henceforth we would be given bread and water only. Upon this fare we continued until September 15.

Saturday, September 14.

Colonel Barnes, the provost marshal, called at the guardhouse. He ordered us to stand at attention, and when we refused to comply, he proceeded to kick the legs of the men. Kaplan had his legs and ankles bruised as a result. Upon leaving he hinted to the prisoners that he would be tempted to pardon them if they would beat us up.

Monday, September 16.

We were again placed on bread and water diet. This continued until the following Sunday, September 22, on which day we had regularly prepared meals, so that between September 7 and 22 we had only two days of regular rations.

Monday, September 23.

We were ordered to stand at attention by the incoming officer of the day and upon refusal we were told that we would be taken out every two hours during the night. This procedure was inaugurated that very night when we were awakened at these periodic intervals, taken out and kept out a while and sent back to bed.

Thursday, September 26.

While walking about in the courtyard the men were kicked and shoved about for not obeying an order to walk in prescribed military fashion — Kaplan and Breger being the particular targets.

In the afternoon Larsen was brutally assaulted, being choked, his head banged against the wall, and dragged around the room by the sergeant of the guards for refusing to clean quarters other than our own.

Friday, September 27.

Again, while exercising, the men were grossly maltreated. The bayonet was applied to all of us. Larsen receiving a scar. Kaplan and Breger were beaten with the butt end of the rifle. All were kicked and shoved about.

Eight conscientious objectors came here from the Fort Riley guardhouse. [I was one of them. –M.S.]

After supper we were ordered outside where we formed in double rank. The sergeant of the guards issued some military commands to us. When we did not obey promptly, he shoved us about violently. We then began marching around the building. Orders were given to "double time." Bayonets were pressed against the bodies of Larsen, Silver, and others to obtain compliance, but no one ran. The guards now insisted that we walk in strict military posture and cuffs, kicks, and blows were rained upon those who failed to do so. Eichel refused to submit to this abuse and informed the guard that since in his opinion exercise was optional with conscientious objectors, he would march no more under such brutal impositions. A guard seized him by the neck and forced him around the building, heaping blows and kicks upon him at the same time. When he was finally released the back of his head was covered with bumps and he was sore all over.

At about 9 that evening we were again ordered out and again put through the same ordeal. This time Steiner ceased walking. He was seized by the ears and dragged around the building. Another guard after a while seized him by the throat and choked him so forcibly that he sank breathless to the ground. Steiner reported his treatment to the officer of the day, a second lieutenant, who refused to give his name and insisted that he was carrying out orders.

We were informed that we would be called out every two hours. At 11 p.m. we were awakened and ordered out. We refused. It was debated whether or not to forcibly drag us out. They finally decided to leave us alone. However, none could sleep, for the thought that we might be roused any moment kept preying upon our minds.

Saturday, September 28.

At 8:30 p.m. the sergeant of the guards ordered us out. Expecting a repetition of yesterday's affair, especially so since the sergeant was a veritable brute, we refused. Kaplan, half undressed, was the first to rouse his venom. He was lifted bodily off his bed and thrown against the bedstead so forcibly that his skull might have been smashed. He was then ordered to put on his shoes. He refused. The sergeant seized him and put him out barefooted. The other men were similarly handled.

When we were finally lined up outside, the sergeant following us out — and never did man gloat so over his accomplishment — he remarked that he was carrying out the major's orders, meaning Major Taussig, the military police officer. After marching around a while, we were permitted to return to quarters. Threats of subsequent and periodic repetition of this treatment again had the effect of keeping us awake and expectant all night.

The instructions that conscientious objectors are to be permitted to exercise are being utilized as a means to impose hardships upon us. We are kept outdoors in all sorts of weather, from six to eight hours each day, and the guards are instructed to see to it that we keep moving continually. This is a source of constant irritation and friction between us and the guards, for some of us find it physically impossible to keep walking all day.

Our correspondence privilege has been restricted to one letter a week. The letter must be written upon one side of one small sheet. Its contents are subjected to careful censorship.

A general and thorough raid was made upon our quarters for books, magazines, and other reading matter.

All prisoners were ordered to take a cold shower.

Friday, October 4.

Orders were issued that conscientious objectors are not to be given but one helping of food and "damned little at that." Not even an extra piece of bread is allowed us. We are kept hungry from meal to meal.

Saturday, October 5.

We were ordered to take a cold shower. Da Rosa, feeling that cold showers are detrimental to him and having taken a bath but one half-hour previous to the issuing of the above order, refused to undress. The corporal of the guards thrust him under the spray with his clothes on. Da Rosa returned to the guard room, wearing his dripping clothes. The colonel ordered him to undress and take a thorough shower. When Da Rosa again refused, the corporal tore his clothes from his body and at the same time delivered upon him some telling and effective blows. He was then placed under the cold shower.

We were compelled to take a cold shower once in the morning and once in the afternoon. A guard stood watch and checked each man.

Sunday, October 6.

In the afternoon, Sandin collapsed while taking his second cold shower of the day. We explained to the doctor who called the nature of the treatment we had been receiving lately. We also informed him that we were being underfed.

The captain, who was "officer of the day," ordered that we be deprived of supper because we did not stand at "attention" at roll-call.

At midnight we were suddenly and unexpectedly roused by the sergeant of the guards and ordered to take a cold shower. It was obvious that this was an unreasonable and vicious imposition and most of us refused to get up. We were then violently dragged into the shower room and held underneath the spray, night clothes and all, until thoroughly exhausted. Kaplan, Breger, Block, Powell, Franklin, Eichel, Downey, Steiner, and Da Rosa were so treated. The "officer of the day" was present and directed the proceedings.

Monday, October 7.

Greenberg, Block, Bernstein, and others have gone on sick report this morning, suffering from colds. Block and Bernstein were given aspirin tablets to make them perspire. Though the day was rainy and damp, all hands were ordered out for exercise. We were kept outside in the drizzle, until ordered to come in for a cold shower. Even those who have taken aspirin tablets were not excused from the prescribed bath.

Breger, Monsky, Ott, Silver, Da Rosa, Block, and Eichel have already declared an absolute hunger-strike as a vehement protest against this treatment.

Another cold shower was administered to us in the afternoon. At 8 p.m. the "officer of the day," a captain, and the sergeant of the guards ordered all to undress in the squadron and prepare for a cold shower, the third that day. We were marched to the latrine in a body. The captain himself brought forth scrub brushes, used ordinarily for cleaning toilet seats and brooms used for sweeping, and ordered that we scrub each other with them. Franklin refused to use the filthy brush. He was seized and roughly thrown to the cement floor, dragged back and forth and viciously belabored until thoroughly exhausted, he was then placed under the cold spray and left there until he collapsed. Eichel and Shotkin helped him back to his bed. When he recovered, he became hysterical.

The captain wished to know what had happened. Eichel explained that Franklin was suffering from myocarditis and the constant and frequent imposition of cold showers had in all probability aggravated this ailment. Eichel then requested the captain to permit him to see the post commander. This the captain refused to do, although he told Eichel that he was carrying out the instructions of the post commander in treating us so.

Tuesday, October 8.

Franklin, Sandin, and Hennessey have joined the hunger strike as protest against our inhuman treatment.

At about 8 p.m. the order was issued to prepare for a cold shower. Monsky informed the captain, who directed proceedings, that he would not undress. The captain ordered a guard to undress and keep him under the shower twice as long. The sergeant of the guards times everyone. Monsky was kept under the spray an unusually long time. He finally heard the captain say, "If he suffers, keep him there; but if he isn't suffering let him go."

Franklin, because of his collapse the previous evening, was given an extra dose and again collapsed. Eichel again requested to be permitted to see the post commander and again was refused.

Quite a few of the men, thoroughly chilled by the shower, had gone to bed to warm up. "Attention" was suddenly called and those in bed were dumped by the guards and dragged to their feet, half naked. The guards proceeded to place them in military posture. Towels, socks, and ropes were utilized to tie their hands in proper position. Then the captain addressed us. "How many of you will now become sensible objectors and go out to do some work this afternoon?" Receiving no favorable response, he said tersely: "All right, another cold shower at 10:30 a.m."

We were then ordered to dress and go out for exercise. Quite a few refusing to do this were rudely dressed and dragged outside.

Promptly at 10:30 o'clock we were ordered in for our cold shower. Monsky, Block, Breger, Franklin, and Eichel, feeling that this was unquestionably punishment for their refusal to work, refused to undress. They were taken to the shower room in their clothes. There Eichel was again ordered to undress. When he refused, a corporal slapped his face vehemently and dragged him back to the squad room.

There the order was repeated, and when Eichel maintained his attitude, the corporal belabored him viciously with slaps across the face and blows upon the head. He was taken back to the shower room, and he as well as the others who had refused to undress were placed and kept underneath the spray in their clothes,

Hennessey had undressed for the shower and had stepped underneath. No one was paying any particular attention to him. Suddenly he emitted a wild shriek, began tottering and swinging aimlessly. If someone had not grabbed him instantly, he might have dashed his head against the cement. He was carried to his bed, all the time maintaining his wild cries. Presently his struggles subsided and he remained in a state of coma for almost an hour. No doctor was sent for. Ott now asked permission to see the post commander, and was given the expected response.

Those who had taken the shower in their clothes undressed and went to bed. At about 2 p.m. the order came to get out for exercise. The wet clothes were put on the men and they were thrust outside. We were walking around when the corporal informed us that the major (Taussig) had ordered that we walk more rapidly. Franklin attracted the guards' attention first. He was rushed violently against the wire fence, thrown to the ground and his head banged against the rocks. Monsky next received the brunt of attention. The corporal and guard pummeled, shoved, and abused him. A group gathered to watch the spectacle. Amongst the latter were some friends of the active guard. To please them, he seized Monsky from behind and ran him around the enclosure. Then, acting upon the suggestion of one of the spectators, he deliberately strove to step upon Monsky's bare feet. The latter succeeded for a while in thwarting him, but the inevitable happened and Monsky sank to the ground in agony. His ankle had been sprained.

This cowardly act completely unnerved Breger. "Hurray! Hurray for our brave American," he yelled, and clapped his hands vehemently in applause. He was stopped, but he no longer was master of himself. He stopped, took off his shoes and exclaimed: "Here, do the same to me and show your bravery!" He walked on a while and suddenly let forth an uncanny yell and fell to the ground. He struggled painfully, all the time maintaining his gruesome cries. His struggles ceased finally and amid jeers of "He's all right" he was raised to his feet. Monsky in the meanwhile had been dragged all over the ground, his clothes torn from his body, and was practically unconscious.

The "officer of the day" now came upon the scene. He ordered those who would not walk to be placed in solitary confinement on bread and water. Breger and Monsky were the first to be punished. Eichel discontinued walking. He was dragged around a while and then placed in solitary confinement on bread and water. Steiner now refused to walk, and he, too, was placed in solitary. Silver next attracted the guard's attention. The doctor had come, and Silver informed him that since he had not eaten for two days his physical condition would not permit his exercising, and hence he would walk no more. He was ordered back into the ring by the "officer of the day," and when he refused a guard seized him and threw him to the ground. He then lifted him by the legs, to the intense delight of the spectators, and banged his head against the ground. This act was repeated a number of times. Then Silver, thoroughly shaken up, was placed on the restricted bread and water diet.

Breger, in the squad room, again gave vent to the wild paroxysms. His cries and intense internal struggles continued intermittently for over an hour.

Wednesday, October 9.

Steiner joined the hunger strikers because he had been placed on bread and water.

Eichel was undressed and given a cold shower.

Colonel Barnes, the Provost Marshal, called while some of the objectors were taking their enforced exercise. He ordered them to stand at "attention." When they refused, he beat them vigorously with his heavy riding crop. Shotkin was badly hurt, the colonel breaking his crop over the former's ankles, He deprecated the ruining of his stick and implied that the only reason he did not brain Shotkin was that he wasn't worth the trouble. He then addressed the men, before him. "You have declared a famine strike on me. Well, the Third Assistant Secretary of War — your friend — knows it and has instructed that I permit you to starve to death."

Shotkin, limping, returned to quarters. A guard straightway ordered him outside. Shotkin insisted that he could not walk and demanded medical attention. Though the doctor was in the room at the time, no treatment was given him. On the contrary, though suffering intense pain, he was dragged outside and two guards pushed him around the enclosure.

Steiner was dragged from his solitary cell and ordered to walk. Failing to obey, a guard seized him by his fingers and dragged him around. Steiner suffered intense pain, for the slightest resistance on his part meant the pulling of his finger out of joint.

After supper two slices of bread were given to those who were presumably on bread and water, despite the fact that every one of them was on hunger strike. The sergeant informed them, "Not a damned drop of water do you get until this bread is consumed."

Thursday, October 10.

Ott and Da Rosa, both materially weakened by their hunger strike, were forcibly dressed and put on exercise in the afternoon.

Ott was shoved around a while and then left unmolested.

Da Rosa was pushed about, then thrown to the wet ground, punched, kicked and spat at by the guards. He was raised to his feet and dragged around some more. Presently he was dropped and one guard seized him by the hair and rubbed his face in and banged his head on the ground. His cheek and forehead were bruised, leaving two ugly skin wounds.

Then four guards carried him to the shower room, stripped him of what little clothes remained on his person, placed him on the cold cement floor in an exhausted condition, and turned the cold spray upon him. The soldiers then scrubbed him viciously with filthy brushes and brooms. One guard tickled his feet. He was finally brought back to the squad room in a semi-conscious state.

Downey, Brandon, Bernstein, and Kaplan, feeling they could not conscientiously continue eating while their fellow conscientious objectors were being so brutalized, joined in with the hunger strikers.

Friday, October 11.

Brandon, because of extreme weakness, was unable to walk. A guard pricked him with a bayonet, and then the sergeant of the guards pushed him around.

Saturday, October 12.

In the afternoon all the men, regardless of their physical condition, were ordered to dress and go out for fresh air. Those who refused were forcibly dressed and thrust outside. The men, because of their weakened state, sprawled all over the ground while groups of the spectators watched the miserable and sorry sight. At various times during the afternoon Block, Breger, and Silver collapsed from total exhaustion.

After supper the men were taken out of the solitary cells and returned to the regular squad room.

Monday, October 14.

Major Taussig, accompanied by another major, who introduced himself as our investigator, came into the room in the morning. The latter gazed sneeringly and insolently about the room and without much ado dismissed most of the men from his mind as "Russian foreigners." His questioning was confined for the most part to ascertaining the birth and nativity of the men and establishing them as "Pro-Germans and members of Von Ludendorff's third division." He finally asked, with studied irony, whether any man was in danger of losing his reason or even his life. His final remark was, "There isn't a single American in the crowd."

Our writing tablets and what little money was in our possession were taken from us. A special guard was placed over us.

Tuesday, October 15.

Silver was examined by the doctor, and it was apparent that his condition was very poor. He was hardly able to get out of bed. In the afternoon, he was taken out of our guard room and placed in a solitary cell.

Thursday, October 17.

The men felt that the hunger strike had accomplished its purpose, in that brutalities had been discontinued for the past few days, and decided to eat supper. Bread and milk was given us to break our fast.

Friday, October 18.

Black coffee and bread were sent us for breakfast. Such food at this time most of us felt was actual poison for our systems. Hence, with one or two exceptions, we declined to eat this repast. No other food was furnished us.

Saturday, October 19.

Immediately after breakfast Eichel was viciously and suddenly struck two stinging blows in the mouth for failing, through no fault of his, to properly "cover off" for count.

Later, Ott and Eichel were ordered to clean the latrine by the sergeant of the guards, and when they refused the former slapped, punched, and shoved them violently against the wall and other projections.

Monday, October 21.

The major who made the perfunctory investigation Monday, October 14, returned and began calling each man to explain the mistreatments he had experienced and witnessed.

We wish it known that during this tense period we were held absolutely incommunicado. Packages containing food and delicacies, sent us from home at a great expense of time, money, and sentiment, were viciously and wantonly destroyed and their contents dumped in the garbage cans, though we had at no time been told that we could not receive such packages.

The above is only a brief summary of the atrocities perpetrated upon us. The situation can never be described with sufficient vividness and intensity to impart to the authorities a real impression of the mental and physical anguish suffered by us. Most of the mistreatments took place outside, with large groups watching the sorry and revolting spectacle of defenseless men being most brutally punched, shoved, and abused.

While we do not wish to impugn the motives of the investigator, we have reason to believe, because of his own statements and his obviously antagonistic attitude, that the report of his investigation would be prejudiced and not strictly in accordance with the fullest testimony of the men. We therefore feel justified in submitting this report, which we are willing to affirm under oath, merely as a confirmation to his report.

The men reached the Guard House at Funston on the follow dates — and went through the above experiences from the day of their arrival.

September 8th.

Bernstein, Breger, Greenberg, Kaplan, Henessey, Larsen, Powell.

September 27.

Downey, Eichel Franklin, Ott, Sandin, Shotkin, Silver, Steiner.

September 30.

Block, Da Rosa, Monsky.

October 8.

Brandon

A copy of this report has been given to the investigator.

We the undersigned, consider the above a fair and accurate account of our treatment at the military police guardhouse of Camp Funston, Kansas.

Morris Franklin, Thomas Shotkin, Herman Kaplan, Lester G. Ott, Joseph Brandon, Ulysses Da Rosa, Mayer Bernstein, Henry Monsky, Max Sandin, Emanuel Silver, Benjamin Breger, Rexford Powell, David Eichel, Julius R. Greenberg, Charles P. Larsen, Francis Steiner, Francis X. Henessey, and John Downey

Report on 1919 Strike at Fort Leavenworth

J ournalist Winthrop Lane was commissioned by the National Civil Liberties
Bureau to study prisons in which C.O.s and other political prisoners were
confined. His report was published in *The Survey* (a magazine published in
N.Y., N.Y.), February 15, 1919. This report can also be read online in the
Swarthmore College Peace Collection archives or the Internet Archive.

On Wednesday afternoon, January 29, the" first gang," composed
of about 150 prisoners working outside the walls, quit on their jobs.
The guards in charge made only a nominal effort to induce them to
resume work.

This was the first overt act of the strike. In that mysterious fashion in
which news travels through walls and barred doors in prison, the whole
place was soon humming with the exciting news that the first gang had
struck. What did it mean? What were they striking for? How far did
they intend to go? What was to be their method — violence and to
attempt to overpower the prison authorities, or the quiet methods of
simply refusing to work? Would they try to get others to join them?

One of the members of the "first gang" was a conscientious objector.
In civilian life he had been a newspaper reporter and a poet; he was
known as a "radical." That night he held a conference with friends
in his wing. He told them that he had no desire to participate in a
strike for such petty objects as the men of the first gang were then
considering. No one had formulated that afternoon any statement
of what was wanted. One prisoner wanted more tobacco; another
wanted better food; another resented the treatment of Negroes on an

equality with whites; a fourth felt bitter because he wasn't getting his letters from home; a fifth wanted the privilege of writing more letters himself. This absorption in small desires, and utter disagreement of one man with another, characterized the early stages of the strike. Everyone was discontented, many were surly, but only by chance did any two agree upon the causes of their dissatisfaction.

The prisoner in question told his friends that if he did not join the strike with the other members of his gang, his own safety might be endangered. Local Kansas City newspapers, notably the *Star*, had for a week past been publishing wholly untrue articles of the bitterness existing among the prisoners toward conscientious objectors. Realizing that these stories were not true, this prisoner nevertheless feared that their very publication (they were, of course, read by many prisoners) might produce the antagonism described. A single unfortunate accident might turn against the objectors the passions that had already been aroused against the blacks. If he, an objector, incurred the enmity of his fellows by refusing to join the strike, he might be the unwitting means of bringing about a general hostility toward the four hundred objectors still in prison. That night he went to his cell bed resolved to do what he could to make the strike a general demand for something more than extra tobacco and better food. Forty-eight hours later this man, H. Austin Simons, was the acknowledged spokesmen of the strikers.

This was the night, also, of the fire in the quartermaster's warehouse. The flames were discovered at about six o'clock in the evening and soon bore every appearance of getting beyond control. From my porch on a window ledge in the adjutant's office, where my presence was barely tolerated (twice I had to show my pass to be allowed to stay), I saw the whole panorama of the prison yard. Two conflicts were going on — the effort to control the fire and the effort to prevent trouble among the prisoners. These were securely locked in their cell wings two hundred yards from the fire, but six hundred men (the number in some of the wings) can make short work of locks if they go about it in the right way.

Soldiers from the 49th Infantry regiment, temporarily stationed at the post, had been called out to assist in the emergency. Squad after squad of ten men each ran into the prison yard and disappeared in the direction of the cell wings. One could only guess to what use it might be necessary to put them. Two guards, bearing a limp form, came from the direction of the quartermaster's warehouse and entered the hospital door. They were quickly followed by two more, and then by four carrying a stretcher with a body on it. In all, eleven men were taken to the hospital that evening, overcome by smoke or fatigue. Nine of these were prisoners, trusted inmates who had been allowed to help fight the flames.

Sparks flew over the hospital building and settled upon its roofs. Heavy rolls of smoke poured through its screened porches and doors. One sighed with relief as he noted, that it was built of stone, but quickly became alarmed at the recollection that its annex, containing many patients, was of wood.

An officer came running. "I want ten men quick," he yelled, "men who know how to handle guns." The description seemed superfluous, and the men were off in an instant.

As an organic part of the strike, the fire had no significance. In two hours it was practically extinguished, without loss of life but with the loss of approximately $100,000 worth of clothing and supplies. Its occurrence, however, due as it was to the work of two or three prisoners who later confessed, was evidence of the spirit of unrest. Men were bent upon any measures that gave an outlet to their passions. The strain of it must have been very great on the 2,500 men locked in their cells. The fire screwed the tension to a higher pitch, and left both officers and prisoners with raw nerves.

Next morning occurred the first blunder of the administration. Without consulting Colonel Rice, the executive officer ordered that the prisoners be marched back to their wings immediately after breakfast and that they remain there for the morning. This did two things: it told the men that the officers were afraid that something might happen if they went to work, and it gave them further opportunity for agitation.

At ten o'clock Thursday morning, Colonel Rice said to me: "This I.W.W. trouble that we have been fearing has started with some of the men. I am going down to see about it. Will you come with me?" I accompanied him and several officers to the boiler room where about thirty prisoners were gathered together, talking to a lieutenant from the executive office. Colonel Rice pushed to the center and faced the men. He is a large man whose military bearing is nonetheless impressive from being free and easy. To me, who have never been a prisoner under him, his face is generous and kindly. Rice's manner is not pompous, not domineering. He asked what the trouble was. In reply the spokesman said that the prisoners gathered there were not striking. They had no desire to strike. All they wanted was protection in keeping the boiler plant going. That morning, he said, the men had been called sneaks and scabs by other prisoners and had been threatened with violence if they didn't stop working. This naturally frightened them and they had joined in a request for protection! Colonel Rice told them that measures were being taken for their safety and left them with a strong plea that they continue to perform their duties.

From there he went to the sixth wing, where it was understood that several hundred prisoners were especially vocal in stating their grievances. This wing, like all the others, has eight tiers of cells. Its occupants gathered about the colonel on the main floor and hung to the railings of the lower tiers. Colonel Rice thus faced an audience that packed in close around him and rose half way to the celling.

Colonel Rice asked the men to state their grievances. After an unsatisfactory discussion about the quality of the food, Colonel Rice continued as follows according to Lane's narrative:

"Now, men," began Colonel Rice, "I'm not down here to threaten you. That's not my purpose at all. I would really like to get your point of view. I would like to know what you think you're going to gain by your present conduct. I know many of you have grievances. Some of these grievances are real and some are imaginary. I know what some of them are. I know there are men in here who can't understand why they have such long sentences. I know there are men in here who can't understand why they have fifteen, twenty, twenty-five, and even longer sentences, when other men who, in their judgment have committed similar offenses or no less serious offenses, have only two years."

The colonel had struck home. A mighty shout and handclapping greeted this statement. The colonel went on:

"But what I cannot understand is why you think you are in a position to correct it. For aught you know, there may be others who are now trying to correct it. For aught you know, there may be people who are trying to get clemency for you now. I am not making any promises, but these people may be working hard and may have some chance of success. But what are you doing? You are making it so much harder for them by your present conduct. You are fixing it so that even when the time comes when something might be done for you, those who are making the effort will find their hands tied.

"I am perhaps in closer touch with what is going on here than you think. I have many sources of information and I hear much. If I had no other source then the anonymous letters from prisoners that come to my desk, I would know, for example, that you are saying that you are 3,600 strong, that there are only a few guards, and that you can take things into your own hands. It is true that there are only a few guards, but what you forget is that there are 4,000 soldiers in this post, a soldier for every man, and I can have 'em here in five minutes." (General shifting of feet and sidelong glances.)

"Now, I know there are things about this institution that could be better. And we are working all the time to make them better. I know the service in the dining room is not all that I would like to have it. But there is exactly twice the number of prisoners in this institution that we can reasonably accommodate, and that is a condition that I cannot control. I didn't send you here. Don't imagine that I want to keep you. I'd like to get rid of the whole lot of you. You're no comfort to me."

Such was the groping, during the early stages of the strike, by both prisoners and officers, to find out what this spontaneous, inexplicable movement meant and how to quell it. No one knew yet just what was happening or would happen. No one knew how far the movement would go....

That noon the men were lined up in the yard as usual, to be marched out to work. This was to be the final test. Would the prisoners acknowledge their obligations, or would — one shuddered as he filled in the alternative, with the infantrymen waiting outside.

An officer called out the gangs. "First gang," he shouted, and waited for it to form in line. No one stirred.

"There ain't no first gang," came a voice from the ranks.

"Second gang," shouted the officer.

"There ain't no second gang," came another voice.

"To hell with work. I want to go home," shouted a prisoner.

"Third gang," called the officer.

"There ain't no third gang," came from another quarter.

The officer folded his sheet and, turning to Colonel Rice, remarked that the prisoners of the United States Disciplinary Barracks seemed to be on strike.

Colonel Rice stepped forward. He raised his voice and asked the men to tell him why they refused to work. Again, he pleaded for individuals to come out and tell him what was the trouble. "I want your point of view," he said. "No one will be punished for coming out and speaking to me here. I know you have leaders and I want those leaders to come forth and speak to me, man to man."

No one moved. Two thousand prisoners stood with their arms folded, motionless except for the occasional shouting of individuals. In their ill-fitting coats and shapeless trousers with white numbers two and a half inches high sewed above each knee and across their backs, they looked like what in the eyes of the law they were — a herd of branded criminals. Yet among them were many men of character and attainments, many ignorant youths who had got into trouble through sheer carelessness, many men who had committed offenses for which any civil court would punish them. What could such a conglomerate group have in common!

"We want to go home," shouted some. "We want better food," shouted others. One man brought a laugh by bawling at the top of his lungs: "Give us liberty or give us death!"

Colonel Rice walked up and down, now addressing several sentences at a time to the men, now begging individuals to come forth. Yet no one wanted to reveal himself as a leader in the presence of half a dozen prison officers. Few smiled for though they were suddenly realizing the proportions of their own mass movement, they did not know how to control it or give it direction.

Suddenly the ranks opened and a small prisoner with closely shaven head and wearing a long, ugly raincoat pushed forward. With his intent expression he had somewhat the appearance of a Franciscan monk. I had seen him at the Atlantic branch of the Disciplinary Barracks at Fort Jay and knew him to be the close friend and legal ward of a man long prominent in social work. An officer called: "Here is a speaker sir." There was a quick hush. Beginning in a low voice, the prisoner said:

"Sir, I have been here only a few days. I was transferred four days ago from the Disciplinary Barracks at Fort Jay. I am in no sense a leader of these men. I can speak for myself, however, and (here he raised his voice so that he could be heard throughout the yard), I think I can speak for many others in these silent ranks when I say that our object in thus seeming to oppose authority is that this the only way in which we can make articulate our demand to know what is to become of us. What, sir, is the government going to do with us?"

"I am a conscientious objector. I realize that in thus separating myself from this mass I make myself a marked man among your officers. I am willing to do this, sir, if I can enlighten you, and through you others, in regard to the meaning of this protest. My own sentence happens to be twenty years, but my case is only one. There are hundreds of men in this prison bearing sentences of fifteen, twenty and twenty-five years (I am not now speaking of objectors only) who were new to military methods and requirements, and who committed offenses for which the peace-time judgments would be only a few months or at the most two or three years. Are those men to remain here for the rest of their lives?

"Sir, the armistice was signed nearly three months ago. The war is over, the government has already released 113 of our fellows. Has it not had time to investigate the justice of other claims? You ask, sir, what are our grievances? I answer that this is our grievance. These men, as I read them, intend no violence. You see them here with their arms folded, refusing to work. That is the method of their protest. We ask, and we ask of you because you are the one immediately in authority over us, what is our future?

"In remarks you have just made you have cleared the air more than in your talks yesterday in the wings. At least we may now guess where you stand. But we recognize that your authority is limited. And we wish our protest and our inquiry to be carried over these walls and to reach the seat of authority in Washington. We ask this question and we adopt this method because we are prisoners and because this is the only method known to us."

The prisoner, W. Oral James, stepped back into his place. It was evident that his remarks had made a deep impression upon one part of his audience at least — his fellow prisoners. Colonel Rice spoke briefly in reply, and when he had finished his officers again walked up and down the ranks inviting those who were willing to work to fall out. A hundred did so. The rest stood as before, with arms folded. There were smiles on their faces now. One felt that indecision had vanished and that at last they knew what they were striking for.

The men were marched back to their wings. What was to be done? The number of strikers was about 2,300. They were still part of the military forces of the country. They were subject to military discipline. Their officers were military men. Their conduct was mutiny, and for mutiny there is only one recourse.

That afternoon Colonel Rice telephoned to Major-General Leonard Wood in Chicago for permission to use the soldiers of the 49th Infantry regiment, if he should need them. General Wood issued permission for the use of the troops "to maintain discipline, to protect prisoners and to protect government property." Authority could not be broader. That night when I left the prison to go to supper, I passed the khaki and steel of a thousand soldiers waiting outside the prison gate.

Meanwhile the men had profited by the scene in the yard that noon. The rest of Thursday was the period of actual organization. It was literally true that while the soldiers were being sent for and were marching toward the gate, the strike was gathering the force — and the direction — that carried it through to victory. Organization was first perfected in the seventh wing. a committee was elected and a statement of demands drawn up. The prisoners in this wing sent messages to those in other wings, telling them what the demands were and urging them to elect their own committees, with one prisoner to serve on a general committee that would attempt to confer with the officials. "We urge you to preserve order, to stand firm and commit no violence," concluded the message sent to these wings.

The next morning no attempt was made to take the men out to work. Using my pass I visited the men in the seventh wing. They received me as every body of men who think themselves unjustly treated receives a reporter — with open arms. To them I was bridge to the outside world. One prisoner suggested that I might be a government spy, but he was quickly silenced by those who thought they knew better. After all, they went largely on faith, for only one man in all these hundreds had known me personally before I had arrived a week earlier.

The men were just about to hold a meeting — the "soviet of the seventh wing," they were humorously calling themselves. Simons mounted a box and I leaned over the rail of the first balcony so that I could see the faces both above and below.

Simons was persuasive, eloquent, direct. His periods were rounded, his sentences complete, his climaxes effective. He told them that the strike had been organized in the other wings, each wing having elected a committee just as the seventh had done. He read the demands that had been formulated the night before: (1) that the commandant recommend to the War Department the immediate release of all military prisoners; (2) immunity from punishment for all men who had led in the strike movement; (3) recognition of a permanent grievance committee of prisoners.

He told them that theirs was the just cause of self-government now being fought for throughout the civilized world. He brought prolonged applause by his dramatic announcement that the disciplinary battalion (the group of men about to be restored to the service) had joined the strike, and though this news later proved to be untrue, the reception accorded it showed how eagerly the men welcomed additions to their ranks. He declared that no authority could withstand the power of a united body of men. Efforts, he said, would be made to separate them.

"When the officials come to take you out of your wings," he shouted, "use no violence. Whether they take you out together, in groups, or singly, go quietly into the yard. Once there, refuse to work. Violence accomplishes nothing. Solidarity accomplishes all things. The watchword of the working-men throughout the world today is solidarity. Say nothing, do nothing, but stand like this." The speaker folded his arms. "A man who commits no overt act, but stands like this, is immovable."

As he spoke, I thought of the thousand soldiers outside. I thought of the thick walls that shut these men in, and of the barred doors between them and their fellows. I wondered what was the mysterious power by which the speaker and his listeners thought they could control their own destinies. There seemed a grim and tragic humor in the situation of these upturned faces, eagerly drinking in the word of their interpreter. I wondered if either he or they fully sensed the dire possibilities that seemed so imminent to me.

I returned to the prison offices with this question in my mind. There I learned that Colonel Rice, after a sleepless night had made up his mind. He called me into his office and asked me to sit down. I could see at once that his struggle had been intense. He went quickly to the heart of his decision. He had enough force at his command, he said, to compel obedience from every prisoner. "No one knows better than I," he declared, "what this might mean. It might mean violence and it might mean bloodshed. If these men were merely mutinous, I should not hesitate. But this is no ordinary prison uprising. These men have some justification, much justification, for their feeling of discontent. I know the approved military method of handling this situation, but I know, too, that we are in a changed world today. The American people do not stand for the use of military force if there is a better way. I propose to find that better way. I shall listen to a committee of prisoners. If this is surrender, let them make the most of it."

I felt that he had reached a momentous decision. A moment later I realized just how courageous his decision was. An officer of Colonel Rice's staff stopped me and said:

"Do you know how to settle this mutiny?"

"No" I answered.

"'Well, I do,' he snapped. "I could settle it in seventy-two hours. I'd lock every prisoner in his cell and I'd starve him, that's what I'd do. In three days every one of 'em would be crawling to me on their bellies, begging to be allowed to work. A week'd see them. I'm plumb disgusted with this pusillanimous way of handling a bunch of criminals."

The committee met with the commandant and several other officers at 2:30 that afternoon. When the seventeen prisoners marched into the room, Colonel Rice asked them if they had a spokesman. Simons stepped forward. He said:

"Sir, on behalf of the general prisoners confined in this barracks, I am authorized to present to you the following statement of demands, which I shall read:

"We the men now confined in the U.S.D.B., Fort Leavenworth, Kansas, having been convicted by court-martial, present the following as essential for the restoration of normal conditions:

1. That the commandant immediately release from solitary confinement all men now there for having participated in this movement from its beginning, and that he promise that no man involved in this movement shall be punished or discriminated against in the future for his part in it.

2. That the following telegram be sent to the Secretary of War at once:
"General prisoners confined in the U.S.D.B., Fort Leavenworth,

petition, with approval of commandant, for amnesty to all convicted by court-martial. Senators Chamberlain and Borah, American Bar Association and public opinion generally declare sentences unjust and amnesty the proper redress. Our release is just as urgent as that of the 113 conscientious objectors recently discharged. Democratic military justice requires amnesty. (Signed) Prisoners' General Committee elected at request of officers.

3. That the commandant recognizes a permanent grievance committee to be elected by the men; and that this committee shall have the right to discuss with the authorities such improvements of conditions as seem in the committee's judgment to be desirable.

Colonel Rice took up the points one by one. The first, in spite of its somewhat vague phraseology, was well known to refer particularly to white prisoners who had been placed in solitary confinement for participating in the race riots. Colonel Rice told the committee that eleven of the men so confined had already been released and that the cases of the other three were at that moment being investigated by the executive officer. A new man held this position, "Square Deal" Smith, so called from his record of fairness in the navy. After some parleying, the committee decided to present those facts to the men and to seek their judgment.

It was now Colonel Rice's turn to explode a bombshell. At last, he took the men into his confidence. He read a paragraph from a letter that he had sent to the War Department a month previously on the question of excessive war-time sentences urging that they be reduced to a peace-time basis. This would cut many 15-, 20- and 25-year sentences to a few months, or at most to a year or two. It was evident that the members of the committee were greatly surprised at this revelation of the commandant's action. They stood, however, for the sending of the telegram. Colonel Rice offered instead to deliver the message in person, and explained that he was making an official trip to Washington in two days. To this the committee finally agreed. It agreed also to omit the words, "With approval of commandant," since by taking the message in person Colonel Rice gave evidence of his approval.

The third point caused no difficulty whatever, for Colonel Rice immediately said that he would be entirely willing to discuss matters with a general prisoners' committee, so long as such a committee displayed a proper sense of leadership and remained representative of the men.

The men returned to their wings. They were given an hour — all they asked for — in which to report the decision of the other prisoners.

Rumors quickly came back that the committee was meeting with difficulty in some of the wings. The fourth wing, especially, we heard, was insisting that the message to the Secretary of War be sent at once by wire. The reason was not far to seek. The strike could then be continued until an answer had been received!

At last, the committee returned, four hours after its appointment. A new spokesman stepped to the front.

"Sir, I am spokesman this evening, general prisoner 17380, who acted as spokesman this afternoon being somewhat tired."

Thus spoke Carl Haessler, graduate of the University of Wisconsin, Rhodes Scholar at Oxford, editorial writer, socialist, conscientious objector. He continued:

"Sir, I have to report that the general prisoners confined in this barracks have voted unanimously — unanimously, sir — to return to work tomorrow morning and to restore a normal state of affairs upon the conditions agreed upon this afternoon."

A breath could have been heard. Colonel Rice's eyes softened, his face became suffused with emotion, and he said almost in a whisper, "That is very, very gratifying."

The strike was over. The democratic, non-military method had won. And the members of the 49th Infantry, who had been cooling their heels outside the gates for two days, were sent packing.

Organizations

American Federation of Labor (AFL), a federation of labor unions founded by an alliance of craft unions in Columbus, Ohio, in 1886. It merged with the Congress of Industrial Organizations in 1955 to form the AFL-CIO.

Catholic Worker, a collection of autonomous communities founded by Dorothy Day and Peter Maurin in the United States in 1933 to "live in accordance with the justice and charity of Jesus Christ" with a guiding principle of providing hospitality towards the poor.

Central Committee for Conscientious Objectors (CCCO), founded by a coalition of peace and civil liberties groups to support and offer counseling to conscientious objectors and draft and military resisters, 1948-2010

Church of Brethren, one of the historic peace churches.

Civilian Works Administration (1933-34), a job program established by the New Deal during the Great Depression to create mostly manual-labor jobs for millions of unemployed workers.

Committee for Nonviolent Action (CNVA), formed in 1957 to resist the U.S. government's program of nuclear weapons testing and was one of the first organizations to employ nonviolent direct action to protest the nuclear arms race; merged with War Resisters League in 1967.

Communist Party USA (CPUSA), established in 1919 after a split in the Socialist Party of America following the Russian Revolution; based in New York City.

Doukhobors, a Christian group of Russian origin, known for their pacifism and tradition of oral history, hymn-singing, and verse. They reject the Russian Orthodox priesthood and associated rituals, believing that personal revelation is more important than the Bible. Facing persecution, many migrated to Canada a century ago (Wikipedia).

Fellowship of Reconciliation, an interfaith peace and justice organization based in New York and founded in 1914 to support the rights of conscience in resistance to war and military conscription; published *The World Tomorrow,* 1918–1934.

Hutterites (Hutterite Brethren), a communal, pacifist branch of Anabaptists who trace their roots to the Radical Reformation of the early 16th century.

Industrial Workers of the World (IWW), an international labor union that was founded in Chicago in 1905 with ties to socialist and anarchist labor movements.

International Workers Order (IWO, 1930-1954) a Jewish mutual benefit society with Communist affiliations that broke away from the Workmen's Circle; IWO provided unemployment insurance, medical insurance, and life insurance for its members.

Jehovah's Witnesses, a Christian denomination with membership of about 8.7 million around the world; they refuse to serve in the military and are jailed as C.O.s in many countries.

Mennonite Church, one of the historic peace churches with foundations in the German and Dutch Anabaptist Christian church.

Molokans, a spiritual Christian sect that evolved from Eastern Orthodoxy in the East Slavic lands, had some practices similar to the European Quakers and Mennonites, such as pacifism, communal organization, spiritual meetings, and sub-groupings.

National Civil Liberties Bureau, a civil rights organization founded in 1917 and dedicated to opposing World War I and assisting conscientious objectors; reorganized as the American Civil Liberties Union (ACLU) in 1920.

Peacemakers (1948-1992), a radical pacifist organization founded following a conference on "More Disciplined and Revolutionary Pacifist Activity" in Chicago in July 1948; published *The Peacemaker* and employed nonviolent resistance in the service of peace.

Proletarian Party, a small communist political party in the United States, originating in 1920 and terminated in 1971.

APPENDIX III

Quakers (Religious Society of Friends), one of the historic peace churches, founded in England in the 1700s.

Sane (Committee for a Sane Nuclear Policy), founded in 1957 in response to the nuclear arms race and the Eisenhower administration's policies on the production and testing of nuclear weapons; renamed Peace Action in 1993.

Socialist Party of America (SPA), formed in 1901 and gained support from many different groups, including trade unionists, progressive social reformers, populist farmers and immigrants. SPA's presidential candidate Eugene V. Debs twice won over 900,000 votes in the 1912 and 1920 presidential elections, the latter when he was in prison opposing WW I.

War Resisters League, secular pacifist organization founded in 1923 in the United States and affiliated with War Resisters' International. WRL published *The Conscientious Objector* (1939-1946) during WW II.

Workmen's Circle, a Jewish a mutual aid society established in New York City in 1900 especially for Jewish immigrants; gained branches around the country and has been influential in the American labor movement.

Young People's Socialist League (YPSL), founded in 1907 as the official youth arm of the Socialist Party of America.

Workers Party of America (WPA), the legal, aboveground party organization of the Communist Party USA from 1921 until 1929 when it merged into the Communist Party USA.

Index

Page numbers in italics refer to illustrations.

INDEX